BEGINNING JAZZ KEYBOARD

The Complete Jazz Keyboard Method

Beginning · Intermediate · Mastering

NOAH BAERMAN

Alfred, the leader in educational publishing, and the National Keyboard Workshop, one of America's leading contemporary music schools, have joined forces to bring you the best, most progressive educational tools possible. We hope you will enjoy this book and encourage you to look for other fine products from Alfred and the National Keyboard Workshop.

Acquisition, editorial: Nathaniel Gunod, Workshop Arts
Keyboard editor: Amy Rosser, Workshop Arts
Music typesetting: ProScore, Novato, CA
Interior design: Cathy Bolduc, Workshop Arts

Photo credits clockwise from top: Michael Llewellyn; Karen Miller;
Vadim Sokolov, 1993/PNI; Photodisc; Chicago Historical Society, 1995/PNI;
Photodisc; Burt Glinn, 1960/PNI; (Brick Wall) Jasmine, 1995/PNI

TABLE OF CONTENTS

ABOUT THE AUTHOR

PHOTO CREDIT: DAMION POIRIER

Born and raised in New Haven, CT, Noah Baerman began piano studies at age eight. He had his first formal jazz training at the Educational Center for the Arts in New Haven and at Jackie McLean's Artists' Collective in Hartford. He went on to earn Bachelor's and Master's degrees in jazz studies from Mason Gross School of the Arts at Rutgers University, where he also has taught jazz courses. While at Rutgers, he spent six years under the tutelage of the renowned jazz pianist Kenny Barron. He has worked professionally as a keyboardist in many styles including classical, rock, blues, R&B and Latin jazz. The bulk of his work has been as a performer, educator and composer of straight-ahead jazz. In 1994, he co-founded the collective jazz quartet Positive Rhythmic Force (PRF) along with trumpeter Jason Berg, bassist Ben Tedoff and drummer Sunny Jain. PRF has established itself in the jazz world through clinics, recordings and many performances. Noah has also been active in interdisciplinary arts, creating pieces that employ spoken-word poetry, modern dance, theater and visual art. Many of these pieces have been performed with PRF and several have been collaborations with Noah's wife, Kate TenEyck.

00

Track
1

A compact disc is available for this book. This disc can make learning with this book easier and more enjoyable. This symbol will appear next to every example that is on the CD. Use the CD to help insure that you are capturing the feel of the examples, interpreting the rhythms correctly, and so on. The track numbers below the symbols correspond directly to the example you want to hear. Track 1 will tell you how to use the CD. Have fun!

INTRODUCTION

Welcome to *Beginning Jazz Keyboard*. This book is designed to ease you into playing jazz and create a solid foundation. It assumes you have already begun your keyboard training, are familiar with reading music and have experience playing major and minor scales. Several people I've talked to as I've been writing have expressed a similar interest. They say they hope that the book can help to de-mystify jazz for them. They say they've tried to play jazz before, but there is so much you need to know that it is intimidating. When they've tried to ask for help, they've gotten the impression that jazz is some kind of secret club where they can't get in unless they learn the secret handshake. This book aims to counter these problems.

I'm not going to say that jazz is easy, and I'm not going to say that any method book can teach you everything you need to know. What this book can do, however, is teach you the basics. If you understand the basics of rhythm, harmony and improvisation, you are well on your way. In addition to being able to use the other books in this series to learn more advanced concepts, you'll have the information you need to play and understand jazz. The tradition of jazz education is all about learning while playing, listening and hanging out with other musicians. The information in this book should give you what you need to start doing those things. As you move through the other books in the series, you'll have even more information to integrate with your learned experiences.

A few pieces of advice to help you get the most out of this book:
— Play. Playing jazz is fun and satisfying, so enjoy.
— Listen. To truly understand the concepts in this book, it is absolutely essential to listen to recordings and live performances of good jazz. (See page 95 for some hints.)
— Cross-reference. When you learn a new concept, don't just use it on the tunes that relate to that concept. Try applying it to other tunes to solidify your knowledge.
— Be flexible. The cornerstone of jazz is improvisation. Very little is set in stone, and that may take some getting used to if you're not accustomed to improvising. Think of things like dynamics and phrasing marks as suggestions. For most jazz musicians, these things are instinctive and spontaneous. If you hear a different way to interpret something, trust your ears and try it.

ACKNOWLEDGMENTS
Thank you to everyone who made this project possible (including many people who didn't make it onto this list): to Nat Gunod, Dave Smolover and everyone else at NGW and Workshop Arts; to Alfred Publishing; to Collin Tilton at Bar None Studios; to Dan Morgenstern, Esther Smith, and the rest of the people at the Institute of Jazz Studies; to Steve Bennett, Karl Müller, Wynne Mun, Jeff Grace, Amanda Monaco, Damion Poirier, Jimmy Greene, Noah Richardson, Jeff Bartolotta, Roberto Scrofani, Rachel Green, the TenEyck family and all the rest of the friends who directly or indirectly helped me to put these books together; to all my students who taught me how to teach; to ECA and the Artists' Collective for getting me started with jazz; to the Music Department at Rutgers for all their support and training; to Eva Perriou-Varga, Clara Shen and Wanda Maximilien for their expert piano teaching; to Mike Mossman, Sumi Tonooka, Joanne Brackeen, Larry Ridley, Phil Schaap, Ralph Bowen, and especially Ted Dunbar, George Raccio and Kenny Barron for selflessly sharing their jazz knowledge; to my dear friends and inspiring colleagues from Positive Rhythmic Force, Jason Berg, Ben Tedoff and Sunny Jain; to my family, Mom, Dad, Alison, Jennifer, Matthew and Annie for their boundless support and patience; and to Kate for everything.

CHAPTER 1

Review

This book assumes you already have some experience at the piano. You should know how to read music in both treble and bass clefs. You should also have some experience playing major and minor scales and be familiar with the differences between their sounds. In this chapter, a few basic concepts and scales that are used throughout the series will be reviewed.

Notes

Musical notes are placed on lines and spaces of the staff. The *treble clef* is usually used to notate the right hand, and the bass clef is usually used for the left hand. *Ledger lines* are little lines added above and below the staff. By extending the staff, ledger lines provide a way to indicate notes out of the range of the five-line staff.

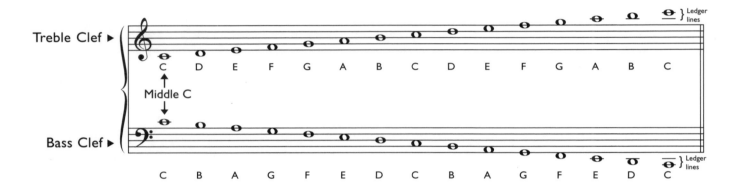

Accidentals are symbols that alter the pitch of a note. A sharp sign (♯) raises the pitch by a half step, meaning that you play a half step (the next available note) to the right of the note that comes after the sign. A *flat* sign (♭) lowers the pitch by a half step, meaning that you play a half step to the left of the note after the sign. Usually, sharps and flats are black keys. A *natural* (♮) sign cancels the preceding accidental. Sharps and flats last until the end of the measure in which they appear. When you go to a new measure, the slate is clean.

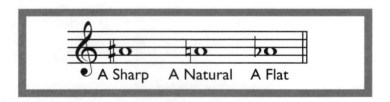

Sometimes there are different ways of writing the same note. Notes that sound the same but have different names are called *enharmonic* notes.

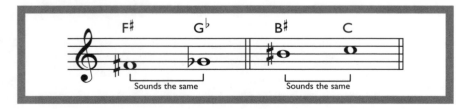

RHYTHM AND TIME SIGNATURE

Once you know which notes to play, you need to know the *rhythm*. Rhythm is a series of various durations. It's easy...if you can count to four, then you're on the verge of mastering rhythm.

A *beat* is the basic unit of time in music. Each note is held for specific amount of time that is measured in beats. For instance, a *quarter note* ♩ lasts for one beat. *Rests*, indicating silence, are valued the same way.

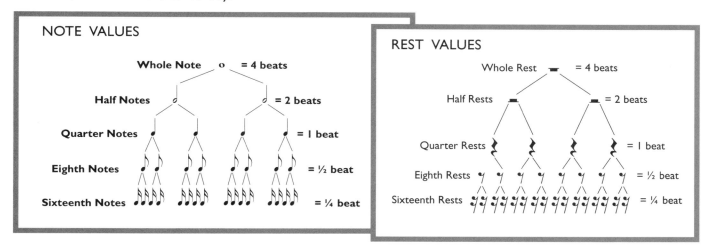

Each piece begins with a *time signature* which tells us how long each measure lasts. The bottom number shows the kind of note that equals one beat (4 means quarter note, 8 means eighth note, etc.). The top number shows how many beats are in each measure.

$\frac{4}{4}$ ← 4 beats per measure
← Quarter note = 1 beat

$\frac{3}{8}$ ← 3 beats per measure
← Eighth note = 1 beat

If you add the values of the notes and rests in a measure, you have the top number from the time signature. By counting the beats you can consistently keep track of the rhythm. You can say "one, two, three, four, one, two . . ." to yourself or just feel the pulse.

A dot after a note or rest increases its value by half. For example, a dotted half note equals three beats.

$$\text{half note } + \text{ quarter note } = \text{ dotted half note}$$
$$2 \quad + \quad 1 \quad = \quad 3$$

If the beats in a measure are divided (with eighth notes, sixteenth notes, etc.), you can count the *subdivisions* or fractions within the beat. With eighth notes count "one and two and three and four and ..." and with sixteenth notes count "one e and a, two e and a ..." to keep track of the rhythm.

An interval is the distance between two notes. The most basic building blocks for intervals are half steps and whole steps. A half step is the shortest distance between two notes and two of these make a whole step. The major scale is made up of this pattern of whole and half steps:

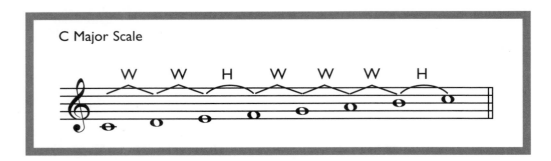

> W = Whole step
> H = Half step

The intervals we use have more specific names, though. Below are the intervals that make up the C Major scale. Check out the number that goes with each note and the names of the intervals.

By counting from one note to another (including the one you started on), you can find the interval that the two notes create. From F to D, count F, G, A, B, C, D - that's six, so you have a 6th. Then there are the other notes, those that don't belong to the C Major scale. Let's see what the numbers and interval names are there.

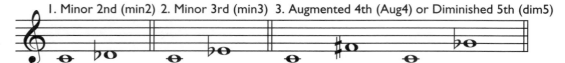

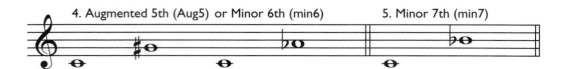

A perfect or major interval that is made a half step bigger is called augmented, and a perfect or minor interval that is made a half step smaller is called diminished. The #4/♭5 is sometimes called a tritone, because its size is three "tones" (whole steps).

Refer to this chart to remember the numbers and interval names based on their size in half steps.

Number	Number of **Half Steps**	Interval	Abbreviation
1	0	perfect unison	PU
♭2	1	minor 2nd	min2
2	2	major 2nd	Maj2
♭3	3	minor 3rd	min3
3	4	major 3rd	Maj3
4	5	perfect 4th	P4
♯4	6 ("tritone")	augmented 4th	Aug4
♭5	6 ("tritone")	diminished 5th	dim5
5	7	perfect 5th	P5
♯5	8	augmented 5th	Aug5
♭6	8	minor 6th	min6
6	9	major 6th	Maj6
♭7	10	minor 7th	min7
7	11	major 7th	Maj7
1	12	perfect octave	P8

Try forming each of these intervals going both up and down from different notes on the keyboard. Play them both melodically (one note at a time) and harmonically (both notes at the same time), and try to learn the characteristic sound of each interval.

INTERVAL INVERSION

Here's a neat trick to quickly figure out some of the intervals. Inversion, which means turning an interval upside down, can be used by remembering that *everything equals nine.*

If you want to find a minor 7th down from C, turn it upside down and go up a major 2nd (7 + 2 = 9) and you get the same note, D. When dealing with larger intervals like this, inversion helps you figure them out by using smaller, more manageable intervals. Take a look at the examples and at the chart below. When inverting, perfect intervals become other perfect intervals. Major becomes minor and vice versa. Augmented becomes diminished and vice versa.

From C: minor 7th down   From C: major 2nd up

From C: major 6th up   From C: minor 3rd down

Interval Inversion Chart
Perfect inverts to perfect
Major inverts to minor
Augmented inverts to diminished
2nd inverts to 7th
3rd inverts to 6th
4th inverts to 5th

As we observed on page 8, the major scale always has the same pattern of whole steps and half steps: whole, whole, half, whole, whole, whole, half. That's why the major scale always has a certain sound no matter what the starting pitch is. Key signatures are derived from scales and tell us which notes have to be raised (with sharps) or lowered (with flats) throughout a piece. Sometimes a scale or piece will be in a minor key rather than a major one. If we play the major scale beginning on the sixth degree of the scale instead of the first degree, the new scale that is produced is called the *relative minor*. The relative minor always has the same key signature as the major scale it comes from.

Look at the key signatures on the opposite page. Note that with the sharp keys, every time you move up the *interval of a 5th* (a distance of 3½ steps) you add a sharp. With the flat keys, every time you move down a 5th you add a flat. This brings us to the circle of 5ths. This circle organizes scales and key signatures in 5ths.

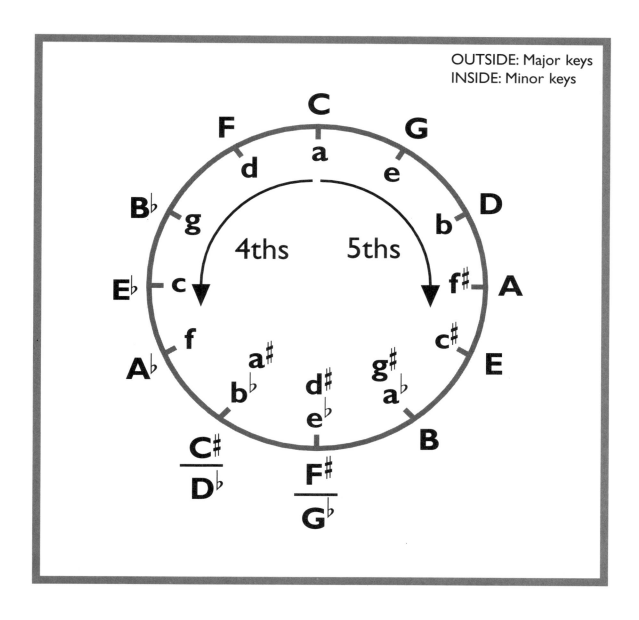

MAJOR SCALES

Here is a review of the twelve major scales. Right hand fingerings are shown above the scale and Left hand fingerings are shown below the scale. Play the left hand scale one octave (8va) lower.

R.H. = Right hand
L.H. = Left hand

C MAJOR (No #'s, no ♭'s)

G MAJOR (One sharp: F#)

D MAJOR (Two sharps: F# and C#)

A MAJOR (Three sharps: F#, C# and G#)

E MAJOR (Four sharps: F#, C#, G# and D#)

B MAJOR (Five sharps: F#, C#, G#, D# and A#)

F MAJOR (One flat: B♭)

R.H.   1 2 3 4 1 2 3 4 4 3 2 1 4 3 2 1

L.H. (8va)   5 4 3 2 1 3 2 1 1 2 3 1 2 3 4 5

B♭ MAJOR (Two flats: B♭ and E♭)

R.H.   4 1 2 3 1 2 3 4 4 3 2 1 3 2 1 4

L.H. (8va)   3 2 1 4 3 2 1 3 3 1 2 3 4 1 2 3

E♭ MAJOR (Three flats: B♭, E♭ and A♭)

R.H.   3 1 2 3 4 1 2 3 3 2 1 4 3 2 1 3

L.H. (8va)   3 2 1 4 3 2 1 3 3 1 2 3 4 1 2 3

A♭ MAJOR (Four flats: B♭, E♭, A♭ and D♭)

R.H.   3 4 1 2 3 1 2 3 3 2 1 3 2 1 4 3

L.H. (8va)   3 2 1 4 3 2 1 3 3 1 2 3 4 1 2 3

D♭ MAJOR (Five flats: B♭, E♭, A♭ D♭ and G♭)

R.H.   2 3 1 2 3 4 1 2 2 1 4 3 2 1 3 2

L.H. (8va)   3 2 1 4 3 2 1 3 3 1 2 3 4 1 2 3

G♭ MAJOR (Six flats: B♭, E♭, A♭, D♭, G♭ and C♭)

R.H.   2 3 4 1 2 3 1 2 2 1 3 2 1 4 3 2

L.H. (8va)   4 3 2 1 3 2 1 4 4 1 2 3 1 2 3 4

NATURAL MINOR SCALES

The natural form of the minor scale contains 8 notes and has the following pattern of whole steps and half steps: whole, half, whole, whole, half, whole, whole. The natural minor scale has a ♭3, ♭6, and ♭7 compared to its parallel major scale. Parallel keys share the same tonic note but have completely different key signatures. For example, A minor has no sharps or flats in its key signature but its parallel key, A major, has three sharps.

A MINOR, relative of C Major (No #'s, no ♭'s)

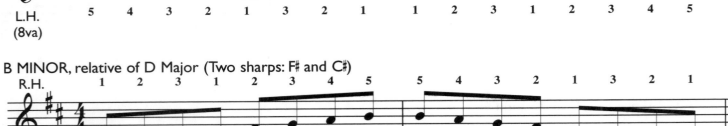

E MINOR, relative of G Major (One sharp: F#)

B MINOR, relative of D Major (Two sharps: F# and C#)

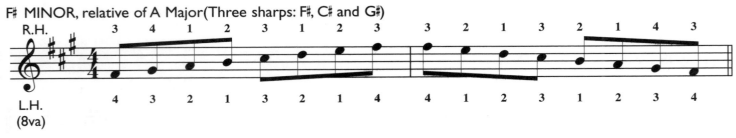

F# MINOR, relative of A Major (Three sharps: F#, C# and G#)

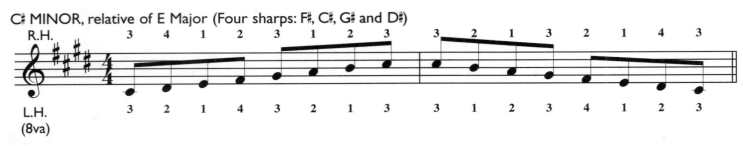

C# MINOR, relative of E Major (Four sharps: F#, C#, G# and D#)

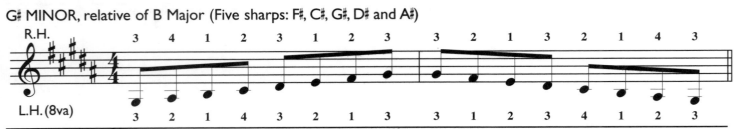

G# MINOR, relative of B Major (Five sharps: F#, C#, G#, D# and A#)

D MINOR, relative of F Major (One flat: B♭)

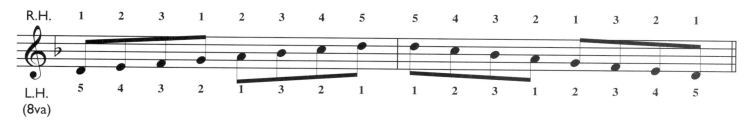

G MINOR, relative of B♭ Major (Two flats: B♭ and E♭)

C MINOR, relative of E♭ Major (Three flats: B♭, E♭ and A♭)

F MINOR, relative of A♭ Major (Four flats: B♭, E♭, A♭ and D♭)

B♭ MINOR, relative of D♭ Major (Five Flats: B♭, E♭, A♭, D♭ and G♭)

E♭ MINOR, relative of G♭ Major (Six Flats: B♭, E♭, A♭, D♭, G♭ and C♭)

HARMONIC MINOR SCALES

The harmonic minor is an important scale. As the name implies, we use it to derive harmonies. It has a raised 7 instead of the ♭7 in the natural minor.

A MINOR, relative of C Major (No #'s, no ♭'s)

E MINOR, relative of G Major (One sharp: F#)

B MINOR, relative of D Major (Two sharps: F# and C#)

F# MINOR, relative of A Major (Three sharps: F#, C# and G#)

C# MINOR, relative of E Major (Four sharps: F#, C#, G# and D#)

G# MINOR, relative of B Major (Five sharps: F#, C#, G#, D# and A#)

✗ = raise note one whole step (two half steps)

D MINOR, relative of F Major (One flat: B♭)

G MINOR, relative of B♭ Major (Two flats: B♭ and E♭)

C MINOR, relative of E♭ Major (Three flats: B♭, E♭ and A♭)

F MINOR, relative of A♭ Major (Four flats: B♭, E♭, A♭ and D♭)

B♭ MINOR, relative of D♭ Major (Five flats: B♭, E♭, A♭, D♭ and G♭)

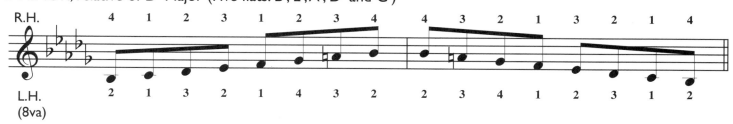

E♭ MINOR, relative of G♭ Major (Six flats: B♭, E♭, A♭, D♭, G♭ and C♭)

CHAPTER 2

Intro to Harmony

Have you ever played more than one note at a time on the keyboard? If so, you have had hands-on experience with harmony. On the most basic level, harmony is anything that involves two or more notes sounding at the same time. Most of the harmony we'll be using involves *chords*, stacks of three or more notes. Guitarists and keyboardists are fortunate to play instruments that allow us to play chords as well as melodies. Some great pianists like Bill Evans and George Shearing are known for simple, sparse harmonies, sometimes using only two or three notes in a chord. Either way, an understanding of harmony is a priceless tool for all of us.

TRIADS

Chords are built using the intervals of the major and minor 3rd. *Triads* are three-note chords. Most Western music you have heard is based on triads. Triads are built by stacking 3rds derived from the scale. To build a C Major chord, use the first degree of the C Major scale, C, the third degree of the scale, E, and the 5th, G. Starting from the bottom, the notes of the triad are referred to as the root, the 3rd and the 5th. In a major chord, the intervals above the root are a major 3rd (C to E) followed by a minor 3rd (E to G). The interval from the root to the 5th is a perfect 5th.

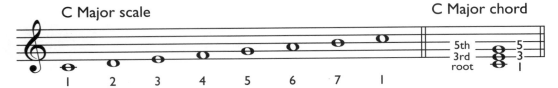

To build a *minor triad*, take a major triad and flat (lower) the 3rd by a half step, leaving the root and 5th the same. The order of the intervals in a minor chord is a minor 3rd followed by a major 3rd. The perfect 5th remains the same as in the major chord.

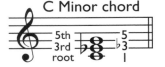

To build an *augmented triad*, take a major triad and sharp (raise) the 5th by a half step. The order of the intervals is a major 3rd followed by another major 3rd. The perfect 5th has changed to an augmented 5th.

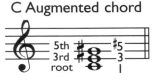

To build a *diminished triad*, take a minor triad and flat the 5th by a half step. The order of the intervals is a minor 3rd followed by another minor 3rd. The perfect 5th has been changed to a diminished 5th.

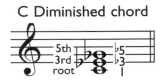

Another type of triad you might encounter is the suspended triad. This is an honorary member of the triad family, not typically mentioned in the same breath as the "big four." The suspended triad has a perfect 4th and a perfect 5th, but no 3rd. The typical use of this chord is for the 4th to resolve to the 3rd of a major triad with the same root, although this chord is sometimes found by itself.

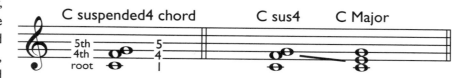

This chart shows the abbreviated symbols which are used to notate each type of chord. In each case, the first symbol listed is the one that will be used in this series. Chord symbols are a shorthand way of indicating what chord is to be played.

Chord	Possible Symbols	Formula
C Major	C, CMaj, CM, C△	1, 3, 5
C minor	Cmin, Cmi, Cm, C-	1, ♭3, 5
C Augmented	CAug, C+	1, 3, #5
C diminished	Cdim, C°	1, ♭3, ♭5
C Suspended4	Csus4, Csus	1, 4, 5

In Harmony will give you a chance to play some triads. Practice the chords first and then add the melody. Look at the chord symbols and notice what chords you are playing.

IN HARMONY

INVERSIONS

The notes C, E and G, form a C Major triad. This is true regardless of the order the notes. A chord with the root on the bottom is in *root position*. A triad whose lowest note isn't the root is in an *inversion*. A triad with the 3rd on the bottom is in *1st inversion*. If the 5th is on the bottom, the chord is in *2nd inversion*.

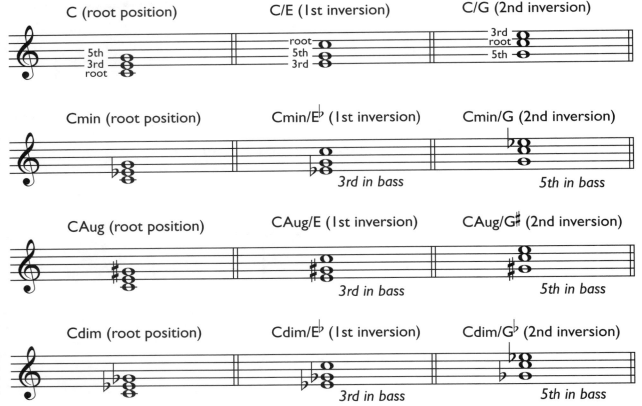

Inverted chords are usually notated as *slash chords*. Slash chords are chords where some note other than the root is the bass (lowest) note. The chord comes before the slash (/) and the bass note comes after the slash. For example, a C/G indicates a second inversion C chord.

VOICING

Voicing is the specific way that the notes in chords are arranged. As mentioned above, any chord is valid as long as it contains all of the notes in that chord. Inversions are used to create smoother and more melodic voice leading. By putting the root in the bass, we can maintain the root position sound. Check out these different ways to voice a C Major triad in root position.

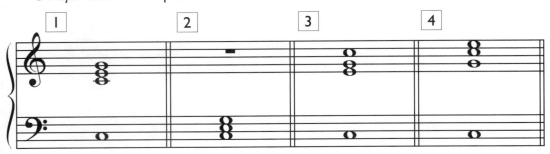

The third and fourth voicings use inversions in the right hand. These are root position chords because the left hand is still playing the root of the chord in the bass. In voicings 1, 3, and 4, the root is played twice, once in each hand. This is called *doubling* that note, and it's fine.

Twilight in Sandy Hook uses inversions to voice triads, and includes a few inversions (where the root isn't in the bass). As with *In Harmony*, pay attention to the chord symbols as you play so you're aware of what chord you're playing at any moment. Play this slowly, at first, to thoroughly hear the harmony, and gradually bring it up to tempo.

Jazz pianists tend to release and depress the pedal as the chords change. This is a little tricky, so practice slowly with the pedal in mind.

Notice the ♩ = 92 marking at the beginning of the piece. This indicates the tempo (speed). Set your metronome to 92, count each click as a quarter note and off you go.

 **TWILIGHT IN SANDY HOOK**

Track 3

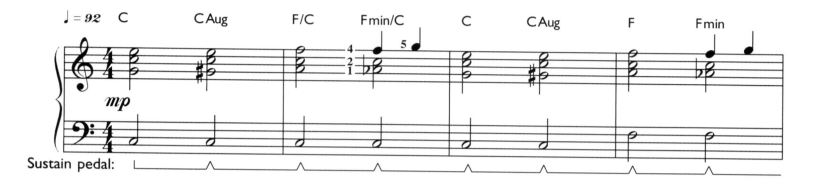

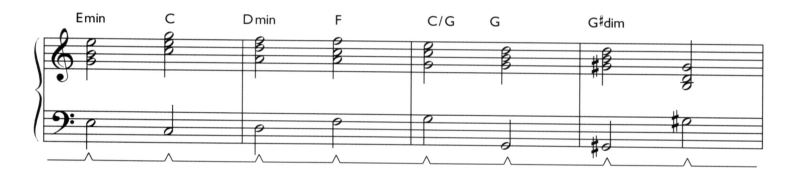

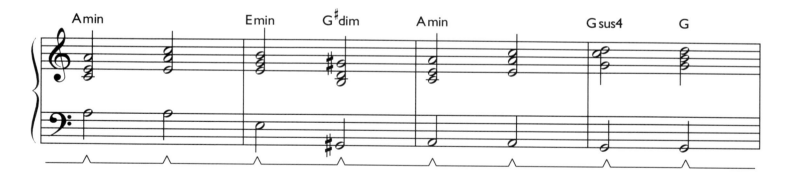

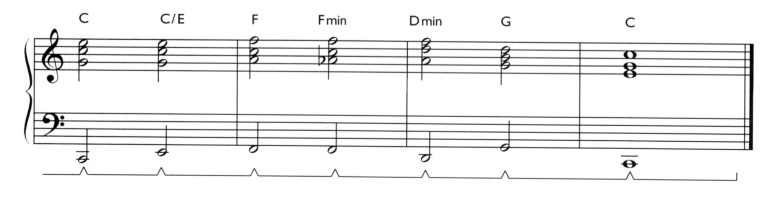

Diatonic means "of the scale." When we refer to diatonic harmony, we mean chords built from a particular scale. The most common way to build these chords is by stacking 3rds from each degree of the scale (through the simple process of skipping every other note). Here are the diatonic chords in the key of C Major derived in this way.

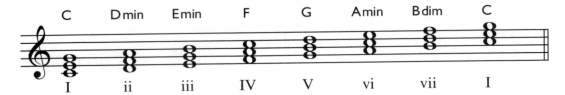

The quality of the chord built on each degree is the same in every major key. We use Roman numerals to signify the scale degree a chord is built on, since that notation is not limited to a particular key (I is I in every key). We use upper case Roman numerals for major and augmented chords and lower case Roman numerals for minor and diminished chords. Here's a quick review of these Roman numerals and their Arabic equivalents.

I	or	i	=	1	V	or	v	=	5
II	or	ii	=	2	VI	or	vi	=	6
III	or	iii	=	3	VII	or	vii	=	7
IV	or	iv	=	4					

In every major key, the type of chord built on each degree is the same:

I	Major		V	Major
ii	Minor		vi	Minor
iii	Minor		vii	Diminished
IV	Major			

When looking for the chords in a particular key, you can refer to the following chart which shows the diatonic chords that belong to each of the twelve keys.

Key	I	ii	iii	IV	V	vi	vii
C	C	Dmin	Emin	F	G	Amin	Bdim
G	G	Amin	Bmin	C	D	Emin	F♯dim
D	D	Emin	F♯min	G	A	Bmin	C♯dim
A	A	Bmin	C♯min	D	E	F♯min	G♯dim
E	E	F♯min	G♯min	A	B	C♯min	D♯dim
B	B	C♯min	D♯min	E	F♯	G♯min	A♯dim
G♭	G♭	A♭min	B♭min	C♭	D♭	E♭min	Fdim
D♭	D♭	E♭min	Fmin	G♭	A♭	B♭min	Cdim
A♭	A♭	B♭min	Cmin	D♭	E♭	Fmin	Gdim
E♭	E♭	Fmin	Gmin	A♭	B♭	Cmin	Ddim
B♭	B♭	Cmin	Dmin	E♭	F	Gmin	Adim
F	F	Gmin	Amin	B♭	C	Dmin	Edim

CHORD FUNCTION AND CHORD PROGRESSIONS

When you see a good movie, you go for a ride. There are moments of tension and excitement along the way but they're usually resolved by the end. If the tension was constant and unresolved, you'd be edgy and tense driving home. Without any tension, you'd be bored. Like movies, music has to go somewhere to be interesting. Movement in music creates interest and excitement when it builds and releases tension at the right moments. A *chord progression* is a series of chords that go somewhere. In jazz we sometimes call the chords in a tune *the changes*, since the change in sound as one chord moves to another defines the sound of a progression.

Each chord in a key has a particular sound and function in the context of the other chords in that key. Roman numerals and the chart on the previous page come in handy as we look at chord progressions. A Roman numeral indicates both the type and function of a chord in a key, and the function of a particular numeral carries over to all other keys. Let's look at the most significant chords for a jazz musician in any major key: I, ii and V.

The leading tone, or 7th degree of the major scale, is a very unstable note sounding like it wants to resolve up a half step to the *tonic* (1st degree). In addition, the ear expects to hear root movement downward in 5ths.

When you play the V chord (or dominant):

1) The ear wants to hear the leading tone (the 3rd of the V chord) resolve to the tonic.
2) The ear wants to hear the root of the dominant chord resolve down a 5th to the tonic.

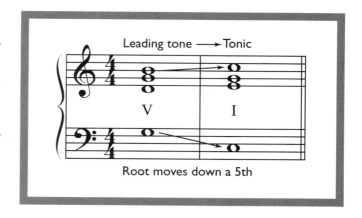

These two elements lead us to the I chord. The sound of V-I is the single most common source of tension and resolution in Western music.

If we use the ii chord before the V chord, we have another instance of downward root movement in 5ths. When the ii moves to the V it's often an upward 4th. By consulting our interval inversion chart, we see that we wind up with the same note and therefore the same effect. The use of the ii chord before the V builds up more tension and intensity, making the resolution to I that much stronger. The ii-V-I progression is the most common progression in jazz. Play the example on the right a few times to get the sound in your head.

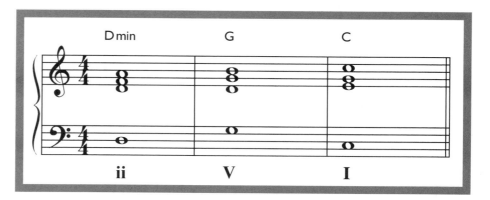

The chart below maps out the basic function of each chord in a major key. Notice that some chords can be substituted for other chords, taking their place in a progression because they have a similar function.

	Table of Chord Functions	
I	Tonic	Home. The most stable chord in a key
ii	Supertonic	Gravitates towards V
iii	Mediant	Can substitute for I (though less stable), or gravitate downward a 5th to vi
IV	Subdominant	Can substitute for ii, gravitating towards V. Commonly used in this way in pop/rock tunes
V	Dominant	Gravitates towards I
vi	Submediant	Can substitute for I (relative minor) or gravitate downward a 5th to ii
vii	Leading Tone	Can substitute for V, gravitating towards I

Enough charts and diagrams for now, let's play and hear what's really going on here. *Ton Doo* uses all 7 chords of the major scale, in this case G Major. Notice how each chord sounds in context, and refer back to the table of chord functions afterward to compare notes between what's on the chart and what you heard. The sound is what will really make the chart (or any other bit of theory) make sense.

TON DOO

Track 4

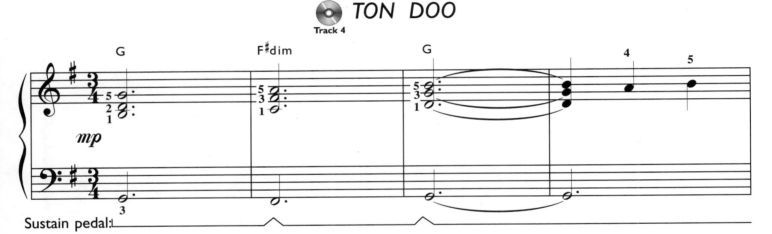

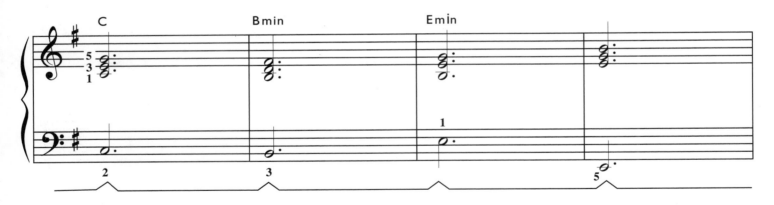

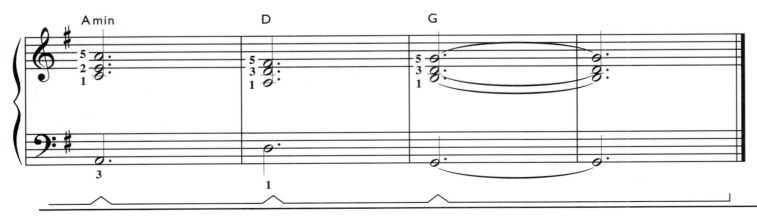

One of the biggest sources of tunes for a jazz player is the "fake book," a book of music that generally crams in as many tunes as possible by giving just enough information for us to figure out what to play. Therefore, we have to learn how to read *lead sheets*. A lead sheet gives us the melody and the chord symbols, and lets us voice the chords as we see fit. As we learn more kinds of voicings, that increases our range of choices as we flesh out a lead sheet.

For example, if we saw this four-bar fragment from a lead sheet . . .

...we might voice it like this, playing the roots in the left hand and using the right hand to play whichever inversion puts the correct melody note on top.

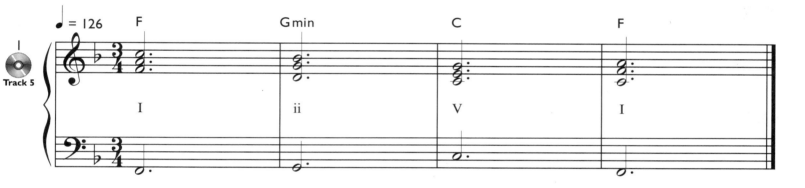

Below is *Ton Doo* in lead sheet form. Try playing through it by just looking at the lead sheet. Form your chords with the bass notes in the left hand and with your right hand play whichever inversion has the melody note on top. In this example, the left hand will always be playing the roots. Once you've tried this, check it against the fully written out version on page 24. Every note doesn't have to match up exactly, but the sound should be similar. Keep going back and forth between the two until you get the hang of it. Notice from the version on page 24 that you need only play one chord per measure, even if there are several notes in the melody.

TON DOO (LEAD SHEET STYLE)

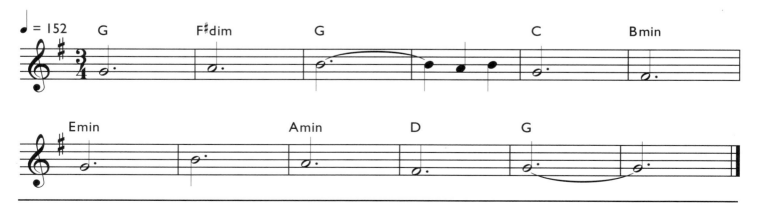

To play something in a minor key, find the relative major key (the one with the same key signature), and borrow its chords, shifting the Roman numerals to match the key.

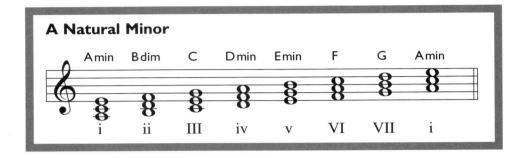

Traditionally, the harmonic minor (see p. 16-17) is used for minor key harmony; the same method of stacking 3rds is used, but with the raised 7th in the picture instead of the usual ♭7. Compare the chords of A Natural Minor and A Harmonic Minor.

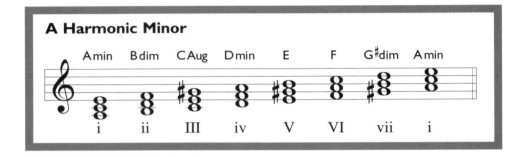

The most notable difference is the V chord. The major V in the harmonic minor gives a much stronger pull back to i (the minor tonic). This gravity pulling toward i is the main reason for using the harmonic minor. In pop and jazz, the two scales are both used, often interchangeably, and where the chords differ, it simply becomes a matter of choice.

Nellie's Woe is notated here in lead sheet style. Try voicing it with the same method you used for *Ton Doo*. The tune is in the key of A Minor, using both natural and harmonic minor harmonies. Notice in particular the difference in the sounds and impacts of the V chords, E (from A Harmonic Minor) and Emin (from A Natural Minor). The next page has the tune written out.

NELLIE'S WOE (LEAD SHEET)

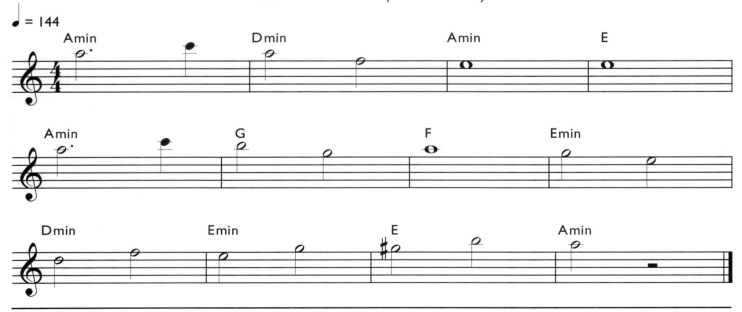

As a reward for your efforts on the previous page, here is *Nellie's Woe* written out fully.
Like you did with *Ton Doo*, go back and forth between the lead sheet and the written out
music a few times until you become comfortable with the lead sheet.

NELLIE'S WOE

Track 6

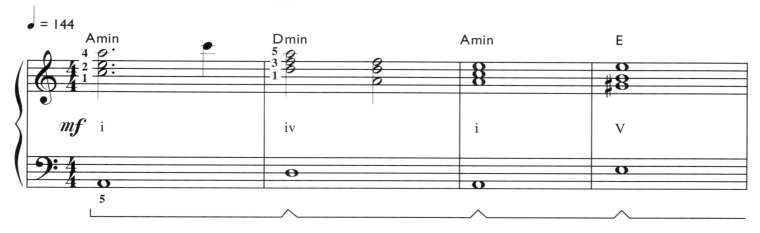

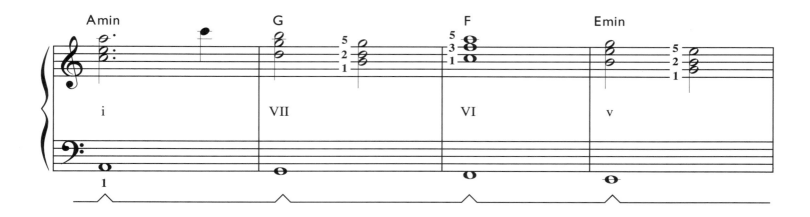

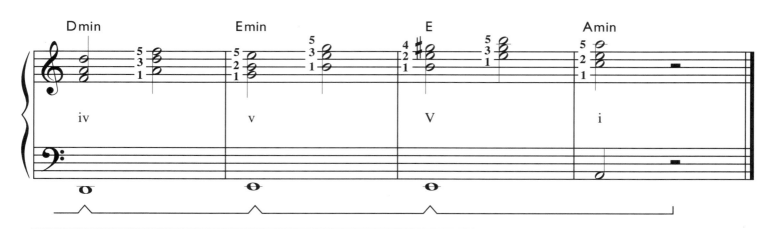

Remember, when playing chords, the pedal can change whenever the chords change.
The pedal does not change when inversions of the same chord are used.

The most common chord progression in jazz (or blues or rock) is the twelve-bar blues. In its most basic form, it consists of three four-bar sections:

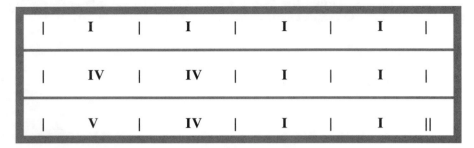

I	I	I	I
IV	IV	I	I
V	IV	I	I

Traditionally, a blues melody presents a four bar phrase, repeats that four bar phrase starting on the IV chord, and then answers it with another four bar phrase starting on the V chord.

> *"I got the lonesome purple blues, blues with a little red. (Sho 'nuff baby)*
> I
> *I got the lonesome purple blues, blues with a little red.*
> IV   I
> *My bloodshot eyes have been cryin' from all those things you said"*
> V   IV   I

Play this progression slowly in a few different keys. Refer back to the diatonic chord chart on page 22 to figure out which chords match up with the numerals for a given key. Once the sound of the progression is in your head, you'll notice how much of the music you hear is based on these chords.

Purple Blues is a twelve-bar blues in F. This time, try playing the chords entirely with the left hand, voiced in root position. The right hand can play the melody. It may be helpful to learn each hand separately first and then put them together. The fully-notated version appears on the next page.

PURPLE BLUES (LEAD SHEET)

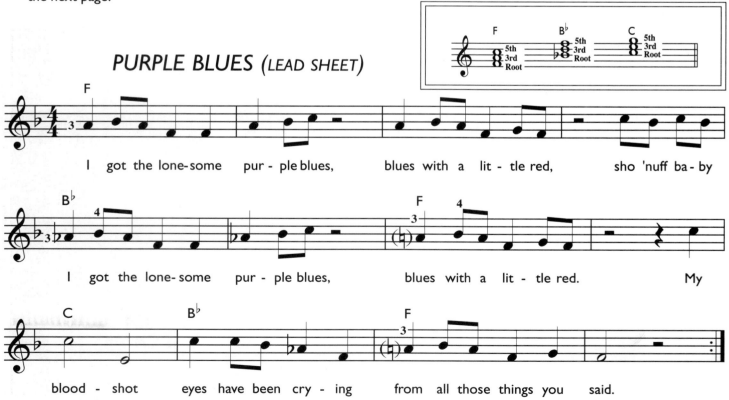

PURPLE BLUES

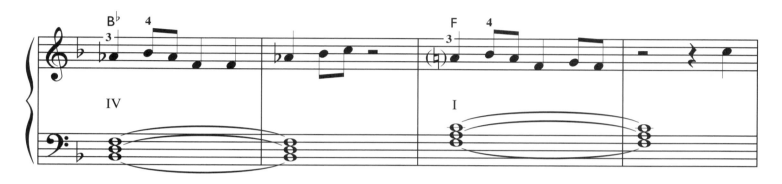

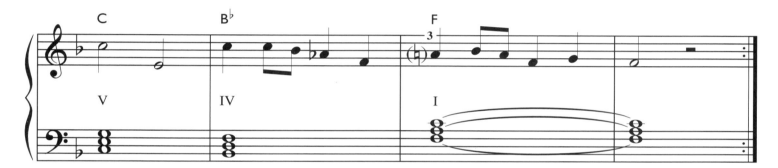

Note:

When playing more involved single-note lines in *Purple Blues*, the pedal is used infrequently (or not at all), as it would make the lines sound muddy.

PHOTO COURTESY OF THE INSTITUTE OF JAZZ STUDIES

*Born in 1894, **James P. Johnson** became known as the father of stride piano. In the 1920s his popularity flourished. He wrote many piano pieces, songs and Broadway shows.*

CHAPTER 3

Feel, Scales and Soloing

It's fun. It's creative. It's liberating. It's expressive. It's in the here and now. It's fundamental to the world of jazz and to life itself. It's *improvisation*! Improvisation is the act of spontaneously playing music, making up the things you play as you go along. If you've ever had a conversation, you have used the skill of improvisation. You can't have a real conversation if you plan out everything you're going to say beforehand. You need to be in the moment and respond to whatever is being said. Your control of the language allows you to spontaneously express your thoughts.

Jazz improvisation is no different. You use whatever information you have at your disposal to put your ideas and feelings into music. This music is generally not pulled out of thin air. Instead, the jazz musician learns a musical language of scales, chords, rhythms and so on. When it's time to "speak," this knowledge acts as the foundation for improvised expression.

The most dramatic use of improvisation is the solo. If you listen to live or recorded jazz, it often revolves around solos. The *head*, which is the basic melody of a tune, is played at the beginning and the end of a piece. In between, you hear some or all of the players improvise solos. The chance to solo is a wonderful opportunity for a jazz musician. Not only are your ideas in the forefront, but they are the ideas that you have right at that moment.

PHOTO COURTESY OF THE INSTITUTE OF JAZZ STUDIES

Earl "Bud" Powell, an important bebop innovator, set the standard for modern jazz keyboard soloing in the 1940s.

STYLE

Imagine a room with four people in it. One is from New York, one is from Texas, one is from London and one is from Dublin, Ireland. All four speak the same language, yet each one sounds very distinct. None of them are speaking more or less correctly than the others, but the accents are different.

Jazz "feel" is like a distinct dialect within the language of music. No scholar is likely to accurately describe how to phrase in a jazz style, but that style does exist. The key is to listen. You couldn't imitate a Scottish accent if you'd never heard one. Likewise, you need to hear jazz to play and understand its rhythms, feel and phrasing. Check out the list of recommended albums on page 95, seek out a jazz-loving friend, teacher or record store employee, and go hear the best jazz players in your area. Soak-in everything you can. The more good stuff you have in your ears, the easier it is to phrase in a jazz style. As you hear more and learn more, you'll begin making choices. You may dig one keyboardist's style and be less into another's. In the end, you ultimately sound like yourself, a personalized mixture of everything you've heard and everything you like.

SWING FEEL

Okay, quiz time.

Swing is:

    a) A popular sub-style of jazz that had its heyday in the 1930's.

    b) A kind of rhythm that serves as a common thread in most jazz phrasing.

    c) A really good feeling that all jazz musicians strive for.

    d) All of the above and more!

If you guessed "d," you are an astute jazzhead well on your way to being righteously swingin'!

The term "swing" was popularized in the 1930s, particularly with big bands. The most respected and popular jazz musicians were praised with names like "the King of Swing" (Benny Goodman), and "the Swinginest Band in All the Land" (Count Basie's). Even as big bands declined in popularity, the feeling of swing remained as a fundamental part of jazz, one that has been there since its early days.

To understand the swing feel, we need to look at the *triplet*. When we divide the beat in two, we get eighth notes. When we divide an eighth note in two, we get sixteenth notes. With triplets, we divide the beat in three. We can count "one-and-a, two-and-a, three . . ." to keep track of the beat.

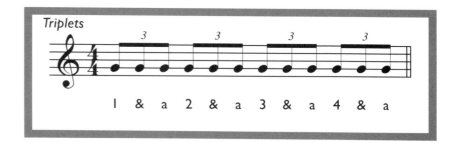

Jazz is usually played and notated using *swing eighth notes*. A pair of swing eighths sounds like a triplet with the first two notes tied together (a tie makes a note last as long as both tied notes combined, without repeating the note).

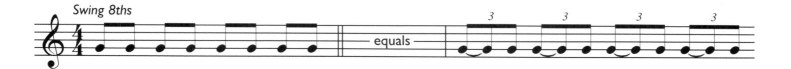

Unless you're told otherwise, assume that all of the following pieces from here on are to be played using swing eighths. Listen to the way different players play their eighth notes. Many old-style players hold the first eighth in a pair for even longer than the $^2/_3$ of a beat shown above, whereas some players play them more evenly. Use the above triplet-based method to play swing eighths, but keep your ears open, too. Like jazz style in general, swing is a concept that is hard to notate but it is very important. If someone says you're swingin', you've just been given one of the highest compliments a jazz musician can receive.

You're about to appreciate the time you've put into practicing the major scale, because you're going to use it to begin improvising. First, practice the left hand part below (a four-bar pattern in C Major) until it is comfortable. Then add the right hand, playing the C Major scale up and down on top of the chords. Repeat this exercise in a continuous loop until it is comfortable enough that you can keep it going without much effort or thought. Remember to swing the eighths.

Now let's try improvising over these changes (chords). Like the exercise above, we'll play up and down the scale as the chords go by. This time, however, we'll try changing the rhythm here and there to keep it interesting (making sure that the right hand doesn't overlap with notes in the left hand's chords).

That already sounds pretty good, but now let's try adding some leaps (notes that aren't next to each other in the scale) and some repeated notes.

Sponge on a Stick is in the key of D Major, and the melody uses only the D Major scale. Once you've learned the tune, go back and try the techniques from the opposite page to solo with the D Major scale. Keep the left hand the same and remember to swing the eighth notes!

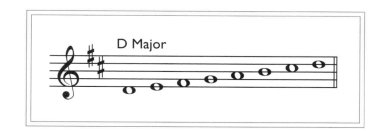

SPONGE ON A STICK

Track 11

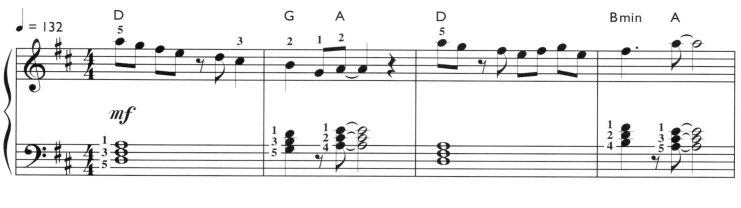

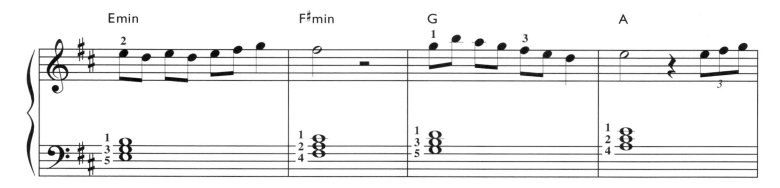

In Greek, *Penta* means "five," and *tonic* means "tone." A pentatonic scale is any scale with five different notes (all the scales we've learned so far have seven). The *major pentatonic scale* is derived from the major scale. To find any major pentatonic scale, simply take the major scale in the same key and eliminate the 4th and 7th degrees. You're left with 1, 2, 3, 5 and 6.

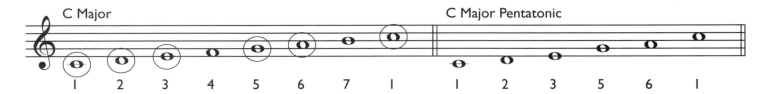

The pentatonic scales are probably the handiest scales for an inexperienced improviser to know, because if you use them over diatonic progressions, it's very hard to play anything that sounds like a wrong note. The pentatonic sound is very accessible. Once you have the scale under your fingers and the sound in your head, you'll be improvising catchy melodies in no time.

Dedicated to pioneering jazz pianist Earl "Fatha" Hines, *Fatha, Fatha*, is in the key of F Major and uses the F Major Pentatonic scale. When you know the melody, try improvising over the chords using the F Major Pentatonic scale.

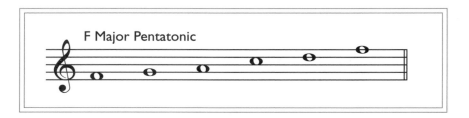

 **FATHA FATHA**
Track 12

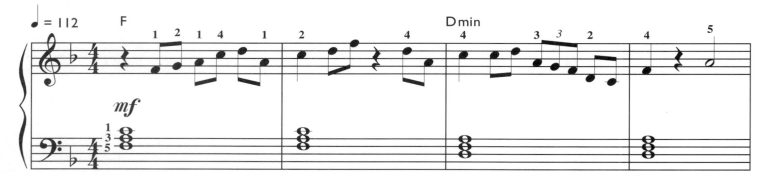

Syncopation is emphasizing the weak beats and weak parts of the beat instead of the strong beats. In jazz that means playing "off" the beat (on the "&'s") instead of consistently landing on the downbeats. Notice the difference below.

In the syncopated example, notice the note on the "&" of four of the first bar (tied to the beginning of the second bar). This is called *anticipation*, because it anticipates the next bar by half a beat. An anticipated note can be tied over to the beat it anticipates or there can be a rest on the beat being anticipated. Either way the ear will still hear the note as relating to the beat it anticipates, but with an added rhythmic bite. When you listen to jazz, be aware of anticipations and other syncopation.

When you're dealing with syncopation, it becomes even more important than usual to keep track of the beat, because the rhythm in the music is less predictable and you don't want it to throw you off. When you encounter music with a lot of syncopation, learn it slowly. Count every beat and division of the beat. Sing or clap the rhythm as you count. Jazz rhythm thrives on syncopation. As you become more comfortable playing both on and off the beat, you will inevitably become much more swingin'.

The example below shows a solo over *Fatha Fatha*. Much of it is syncopated, particularly from the use of anticipations. Take your time learning it. Pay attention to the difference in feel between a note landing on the beat and one that anticipates that beat. Syncopations are highlighted in grey.

SOLO ON FATHA FATHA

Note:

When anticipation occurs, the chord symbol is placed over the beat that is anticipated, not over the anticipated note itself. This helps to keep track of where the fundamental rhythm is.

THE MINOR PENTATONIC SCALE

The *minor pentatonic scale* has a lot in common with the major pentatonic scale. It has five notes, is derived from a scale we already know, and it can be an easy to use tool for convincing improvisation. The scale is derived from the natural minor scale by omitting 2 and ♭6 and playing only 1, ♭3, 4, 5 and ♭7.

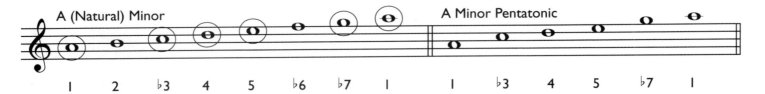

This scale is very useful with minor chord progressions, whether they're based on the natural or harmonic minor. To perhaps an even greater extent than with the major pentatonic scale, it is very hard to play anything that sounds like a wrong note when you use this scale over minor-key changes.

EMBELLISHING A MELODY

One of the earliest forms of jazz improvisation was the embellishment of written melodies. Rather than improvising a melody completely from scratch, players would take a pre-existing melody and change it around — maybe change the rhythm here, add a couple notes there, leave a couple out over here and so on. Let's look at a phrase in G Minor, using the G Minor Pentatonic scale.

Now that we have this little chunk of melody, we can play around with it almost endlessly to come up with new material. Check out some examples, still using the G Minor Pentatonic scale.

Here's *Basie's Minor Boogie*, dedicated to Count Basie. Once again, learn the written melody first, then try improvising over the chords. Try embellishing the melody, and also try improvising completely new melodies. All the while, use the G Minor Pentatonic scale.

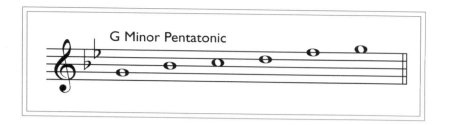

BASIE'S MINOR BOOGIE

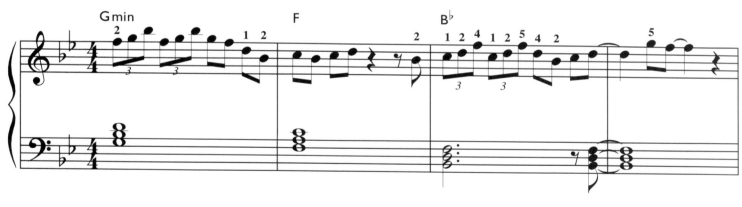

THE BLUES SCALE

In analyzing African-American spirituals, blues, and jazz, certain notes in a scale are called *blue notes* since they are said to have a distinctly mournful, bluesy quality. Some notes are just more blue than others. The notes in any key or scale that are most commonly called *blue notes* are the ♭3, ♭5 and ♭7. The pentatonic minor scale already has a ♭3 and a ♭7, but doesn't have a ♭5. To derive the *blues scale*, we take the pentatonic minor scale and add a ♭5 in between the 4 and the 5, giving us all three blue notes in one six-note scale. To build any blues scale, use 1, ♭3, 4, ♭5, 5 and ♭7.

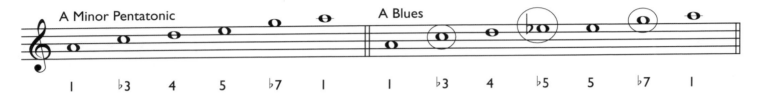

You can use the blues scale in the same places as the minor pentatonic scale: in minor-key progressions. Sometimes you can use it over other progressions, particularly blues progressions, to add a distinctively bluesy, gritty sound. For example, you could noodle over the chords from *Purple Blues* (p. 29) using the F Blues scale. In jazz, blues, and rock music, this scale is indispensable. Some guitarists and keyboardists have built reputations and careers with solos using little or nothing else besides the blues scale. And if you combine this scale with a good groove, it's unstoppable.

TWO AND FOUR

Another key to swinging is recognizing the importance of beats two and four in a bar of $\frac{4}{4}$ time. If you listen to the drum beat on virtually any rock tune, you'll hear the drummer accenting the 2nd and 4th beat of every bar on the snare drum. This is called the *backbeat*. In jazz, the backbeat is generally more subtle, but the players hear it even if nobody is explicitly playing it. To practice, try playing simple rhythms or tunes you know well at the piano. On the two and four, tap your foot or snap your fingers on your free hand (if you have one).

You'll often see jazz players (or hip fans) snapping their fingers on the two and four, a sign that they feel the pulse of the music rocking off the backbeat. Develop your ability to feel and hear this backbeat naturally.

Note:

A common and effective way to practice feeling the backbeat is to set your metronome at half the normal tempo for a quarter note and think of the clicks as the two and four.

Yes, Les McCann Can is dedicated to the great jazz keyboardist Les McCann, who has made much use of the blues scale over the years. And yes, he can play the blues. The melody is based on the E Blues scale. Learn it well, and then try playing it with your right hand while snapping or tapping the backbeat. And, of course, solo over the chords with the E Blues scale.

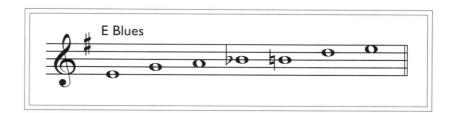

YES, LES McCANN CAN

Track 19

CHAPTER 4

Intro to Four-Note Chords

In Chapter 2, we learned how to formulate triads, three-note chords made up of root, 3rd and 5th. 7th chords are formed the same way but they have four notes: root, 3rd, 5th and 7th. If you're used to triads, the sound will take some getting used to, but 7th chords are colorful, versatile and much more common in jazz than triads.

We can find each of the 5 main types of 7th chords by taking a triad we already know and adding a note.

The *major 7th chord* takes a major triad and adds a major 7th on top. **The formula is 1, 3, 5, 7.**

The *dominant 7th chord* takes a major triad and adds a minor 7th. It is called dominant since it is built on the 5th (dominant) degree of a scale or key. **The formula is 1, 3, 5, ♭7.**

The *minor 7th chord* takes a minor triad and adds a minor 7th. **The formula is 1, ♭3, 5, ♭7.**

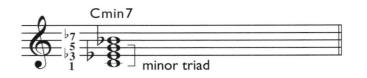

The *minor 7th flat five* (or "half-diminished") *chord* takes a diminished triad and adds a minor 7th. The name half-diminished means that the 5th is diminished but not the 7th (as opposed to the "fully diminished" chord below). **The formula is 1, ♭3, ♭5, ♭7.**

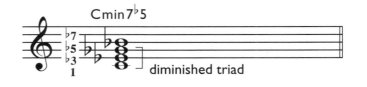

The *diminished 7th chord* takes a diminished triad and adds a diminished 7th. The diminished 7th on top is enharmonically equivalent to a major 6th. **The formula is 1, ♭3, ♭5, 6 (or ♭♭7).** *

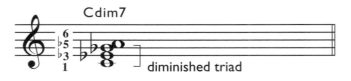

*Rather than use the ♭♭7, we will substitute the equilavent 6th spelling for simplicity.

6th chords are another kind of four-note chord that we use in jazz. Rather than being built as root, 3rd, 5th, 7th, a 6th chord is root, 3rd, 5th and <u>6th</u>. We can find and build 6th chords the same way we built 7th chords, starting with a triad and adding a note on top.

The *Major 6th chord* takes a major triad and adds a major 6th. **The formula is 1, 3, 5, 6.** The major 6th chord and major 7th chord are interchangeable.

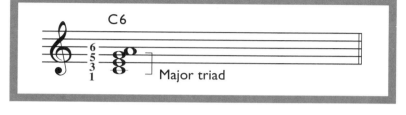

The *minor 6th chord* takes a minor triad and adds a major 6th. **The formula is 1, ♭3, 5, 6.** The minor 6th chord is often used as a i chord in a minor key.

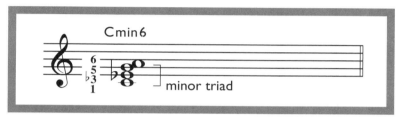

This chart shows the common symbols used for the different types of 7th and 6th chords. As with the triads, the first symbol listed for each chord is the one that will be used in these books.

Chord	Possible Symbols	Formula
C Major 7th	CMaj7, CM7, C△7	1, 3, 5, 7
C Major 6th	C6, CMaj6, CM6, C△6	1, 3, 5, 6
C Dominant 7th	C7	1, 3, 5, ♭7
C Minor 7th	Cmin7, Cmi7, Cm7, C-7	1, ♭3, 5, ♭7
C Minor 6th	Cmin6, Cmi6, Cm6, C-6	1, ♭3, 5, 6
C Minor 7th (flat 5)	Cmin7♭5, Cmi7♭5, Cm7♭5, C-7♭5, Cm7-5, Cø	1, ♭3, ♭5, ♭7
C Diminished 7th	Cdim7, C°7	1, ♭3, ♭5, 6 (♭♭7)

Try playing each of these chords starting on any note. Pick a root and use the formula for each chord to play all seven of these chords from that root. Also, you can pick a chord type and play it through the circle of 5ths.

The exercise below will take you through all seven of these chord types. Play it as written, and then play it an octave lower with your left hand so that each hand gets a chance to play the chords. Make sure to look at the chord symbols and be aware of which chords you're playing.

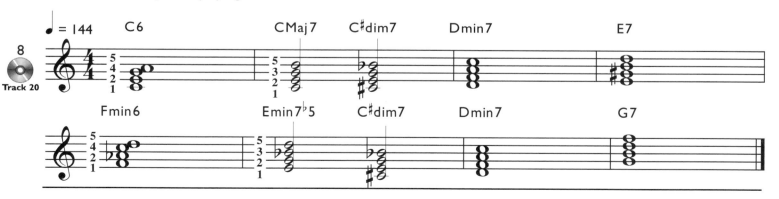

INVERSIONS OF 7TH AND 6TH CHORDS

Inversion of four-note chords is done the same way as with triads, but now we have four forms of each chord. The intervals are inverted too, so you'll notice that the 7ths become 2nds in the inverted 7th chords, often giving the chords an intense, biting sound.

Note:

Notice that the 3rd inversion C6 chord has the same notes as a root position Amin7 chord. Likewise, the 3rd inversion Cmin6 chord has the same notes as a root position Amin7♭5 chord. In jazz harmony, you will often find instances where a single harmony could have several names and functions. This isn't supposed to be bewildering, it is actually a source of freedom. When you're in that situation, the chord can be whichever you want it to be at that moment.

Inversions of these chords, like triad inversions, can also be used in the right hand over roots in the left hand to give us a greater variety of root position chord voicings. This will be your greatest use for the inversions. It is uncommon to find 7th chords with non-root bass notes in jazz tunes, but the need for inversions in voicings will arise often. Here are some examples of a C7 chord voiced this way.

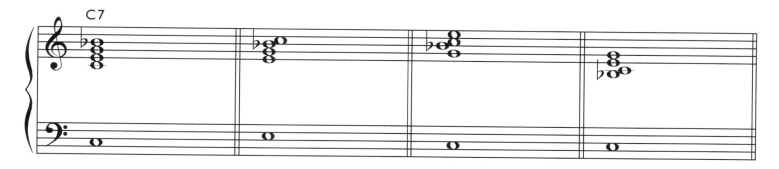

Play *All You Need is Seven* for some more practice playing 7th and 6th chords. Like you did with *Twilight in Sandy Hook* (page 21), play it slowly to get the sound of each chord in your ears and then increase the tempo to get your hands used to the movement. Many of the chords will be voiced with inversions in the right hand and with the left playing roots as bass notes. Watch the chord symbols to make sure you always know what chords you're playing as you play them. The changes are in the style of the standard tune *Don't Blame Me*, popularized by Charlie Parker.

 ALL YOU NEED IS SEVEN

Track 21

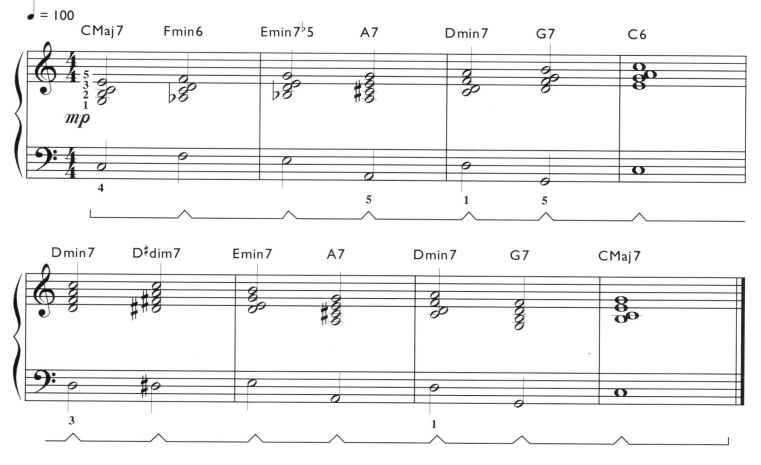

We build diatonic 7th chords in a key the same way we build triads. The only difference is that we stack an extra note on top.

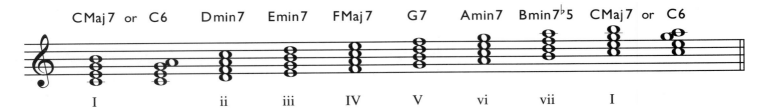

In every major key, the following 7th chords are built from each degree of the scale:

I	Maj7		V	(Dominant) 7
ii	min7		vi	min7
iii	min7		vii	min7♭5
IV	Maj7			

This chart shows the diatonic 7th chords in every key:

Key	I	ii	iii	IV	V	vi	vii
C	CMaj7	Dmin7	Emin7	FMaj7	G7	Amin7	Bmin7♭5
G	GMaj7	Amin7	Bmin7	CMaj7	D7	Emin7	F♯min7♭5
D	DMaj7	Emin7	F♯min7	GMaj7	A7	Bmin7	C♯min7♭5
A	AMaj7	Bmin7	C♯min7	DMaj7	E7	F♯min7	G♯min7♭5
E	EMaj7	F♯min7	G♯min7	AMaj7	B7	C♯min7	D♯min7♭5
B	BMaj7	C♯min7	D♯min7	EMaj7	F♯7	G♯min7	A♯min7♭5
G♭	G♭Maj7	A♭min7	B♭min7	C♭Maj7	D♭7	E♭min7	Fmin7♭5
D♭	D♭Maj7	E♭min7	Fmin7	G♭Maj7	A♭7	B♭min7	Cmin7♭5
A♭	A♭Maj7	B♭min7	Cmin7	D♭Maj7	E♭7	Fmin7	Gmin7♭5
E♭	E♭Maj7	Fmin7	Gmin7	A♭Maj7	B♭7	Cmin7	Dmin7♭5
B♭	B♭Maj7	Cmin7	Dmin7	E♭Maj7	F7	Gmin7	Amin7♭5
F	FMaj7	Gmin7	Amin7	B♭Maj7	C7	Dmin7	Emin7♭5

These diatonic chords function in a similar way to their respective triads (p. 22), with the notable exception of the min7♭5 built on vii. The min7♭5 doesn't generally gravitate to the I chord; its most common function is in minor keys, and will be discussed in a couple of pages.

Play the following tune in the key of G Major, and notice the way the chords function as they lead us away from our home of G and back again. The last two measures are a *turnaround*, a chord progression that creates motion bringing us back to the top (beginning) of the tune. We could just play G6 for those two measures, but by the time we got back to the top, we'd have been "home" for three bars, and might get a bit stir crazy. The I-vi-ii-V progression builds anticipation so that when we get back to the first bar on the repeat, we're more excited to be there.

A JOG AROUND THE BLOCK

Track 22

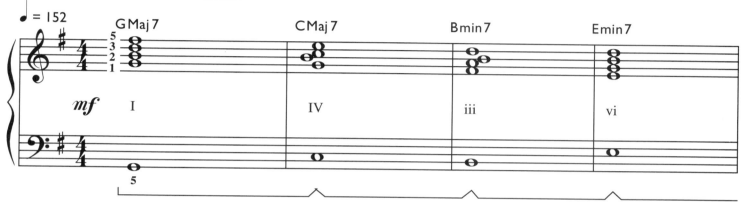

Note:

The pedaling guidelines discussed in Chapter 2 still apply with 7th chords.

*The great pianist **Teddy Wilson** was famous for his work with Benny Goodman, Billie Holiday and Lester Young. In 1936, when he joined the Benny Goodman Trio, he became one of the first black musicians to appear prominently with white artists.*

PHOTO COURTESY OF THE INSTITUTE OF JAZZ STUDIES

When playing 7th chords in a minor key, we generally use the harmonic minor scale to derive our harmony. Check it out in A Minor.

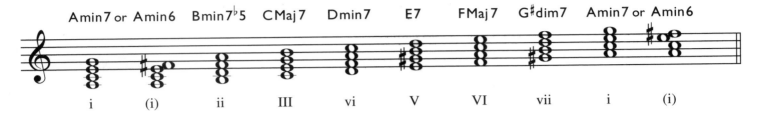

| Amin7 or Amin6 | Bmin7♭5 | CMaj7 | Dmin7 | E7 | FMaj7 | G#dim7 | Amin7 or Amin6 |
| i | (i) | ii | III | vi | V | VI | vii | i | (i) |

What you see above uses some exceptions to the rule of using the harmonic minor. The min7 chord on i is derived from the natural minor, to avoid having a minor chord with a major 7th (a real chord, but one we're not going to deal with until *Intermediate Jazz Keyboard*). The min6 option on the i chord is not from either the harmonic or natural minor scale but is still used sometimes, particularly to prevent clashes between the root and 7th. And the III chord is borrowed from the natural minor. If we used the harmonic minor there, we'd have a Maj7 with a #5 (another chord that is way down the road in our studies).

As mentioned on the previous page, this is where the min7♭5 chord is most useful. On page 23, we looked briefly at the ii-V-I progression (in a major key), the most common chord combination in jazz. The ii sets up the V, and the built-up tension is released as V resolves to I. With the min7♭5 chord as our ii chord, we have a colorful and very useful ii-V-i for minor keys. Check out the sound of the minor ii-V-i in A Minor.

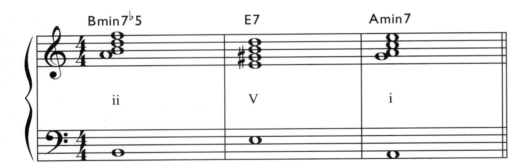

| Bmin7♭5 | E7 | Amin7 |
| ii | V | i |

*Virtuoso pianist, **Erroll Garner** became immensely popular in the 1950s and was the composer of the jazz standard* Misty .

95° in the Shade is an exercise in minor harmony in D Minor. The chords are in the style of the classic Gershwin tune *Summertime*, which has been recorded in jazz versions by John Coltrane, Miles Davis, Sidney Bechet, Louis Armstrong and many others. Once you've played this tune a bit, the minor ii-V-i sound will become a more familiar sound to you. Note that in bars 12 & 13 the chords hint at the relative major key (F), and the final i chord replaces the minor 7th chord with a minor 6th chord.

95° IN THE SHADE

Track 23

CHAPTER 5

Voicing 7th Chords

7th chords open up a whole new world of possibilities. It's funny to think that just one extra note per chord can greatly alter the sound, but dealing with 7th chords does just that. Voicing becomes much more important now that we're using 7th chords. More notes create more voicing possibilities. As jazz keyboardists, we strive to learn what those possibilities are, how to execute them and what impact each one may have on the overall sound.

VOICE LEADING

Play these two examples of voicings for a ii-V-I progressions in B♭ Major.

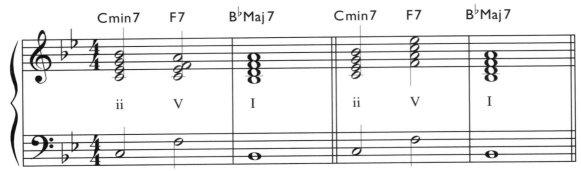

The first example makes more sense. Each voicing flows smoothly to the next one, and the hands have to move very little to play the progression. In the second example the sound is broken up, and the right hand has to jump around to play the chords. The difference is that the first example uses good voice leading. *Voice leading* is the smooth movement of voices (notes) from one chord to the next. If your hands are jumping all over the place, you're probably not using good voice leading, and the music is unlikely to sound smooth or cohesive. To voice lead well, your hands should expend the least possible amount of energy. Imagine that, the easier it is to play, the better it sounds!

Check out this example of a iii-vi-ii-V-I progression in F Major with good voice leading.

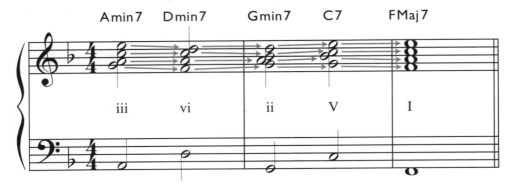

Each of the four voices in the right hand moves very little as the chords change. Just like the individual singers in a choir, who can't jump around too much without getting tired and confused, the voices in a chord should avoid leaps whenever possible. The bass notes move around more but that's inevitable when the roots are moving in large intervals like 4ths and 5ths. Since the left hand is playing one note at a time, it is not difficult to play.

We have more freedom with voicing when the left hand plays the roots. So far, we've been playing four notes at a time in the right hand whenever we play 7th chords. Now that we're getting the hang of them, we can eliminate one of those notes. The right hand can play the 3rd, 5th and 7th of each chord and the left hand can take care of the roots.

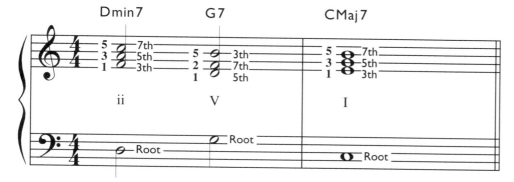

With this kind of voicing, the sound becomes more open. We don't lose the fullness because all four notes of each chord are still being played. We still use the same method of voice leading, simply omitting the root from the right hand. Let's take the following progression in B Minor (the vertical slash marks underneath each chord are shorthand indicating the number of beats devoted to each chord).

Bmin7	Emin7	Bmin7	GMaj7	C#min7♭5	F#7	Bmin7
/ /	/ /	/ /	/ /	/ /	/ /	/ / / /

Let's voice the progression in this style with roots in the left hand, and 3rds, 5ths and 7ths in the right hand with smooth voice leading.

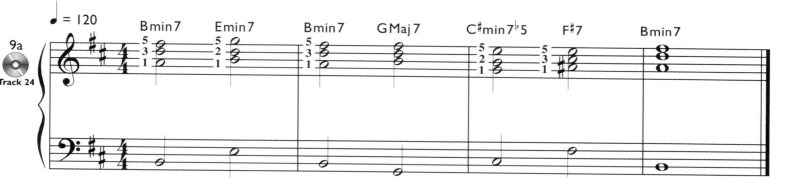

If we begin the progression with a different voicing for the first Bmin7 chord, then the voice leading will naturally lead to other voicings for the rest of the chords, since other voicings will be within easier reach. Here's another way of voicing the same changes with the same technique.

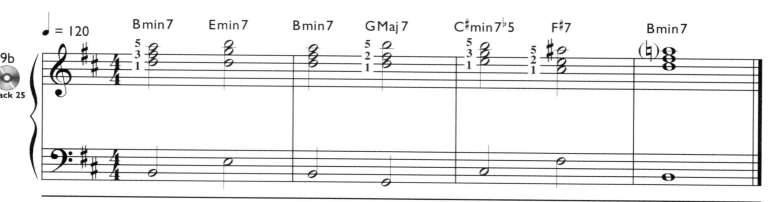

Well, How About Bridgeport? is a chordal study in the style of the changes to *Afternoon in Paris* by John Lewis of the Modern Jazz Quartet. All the chords have the root in the left hand and the other three voices in the right hand. The only exceptions come when the melody note is also the root, in which case both hands play the root and the right hand plays the other three notes of the chord underneath. Notice the smooth voice leading.

WELL, HOW ABOUT BRIDGEPORT?

This song is in *AABA form*, a common song structure where the first section (A-section) is repeated twice, followed by a bridge (B-section), and another repeat of the A-section (*D.C. al Fine). The sum of all this is a *chorus*, which in jazz means once through the entire song form.

*D.C. al Fine (Da Capo al Fine) means to go back to the beginning and play until the *Fine*.

The concept of reading 7th chords in lead sheet is the same as reading triads (see Chapter 2, page 18). You're given a melody and chord symbols, and it is up to you to flesh it out. Once you've chosen a method of voicing (such as roots in the left hand and 3rds, 5ths and 7ths in the right hand) often the voicings choose themselves based on the melody notes.

In this example, the first note is F#. The most sensible way to voice the chord is to put the F# on top, and stack the other voices underneath. The melody note for Emin7 is G so we put that note on top and stack the other chord tones underneath.

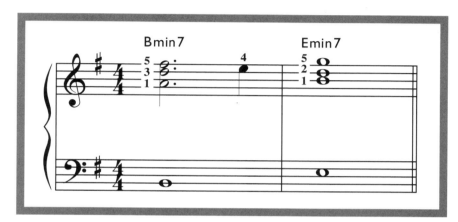

The melody leaps down a 5th at the change to Amin7 so the voicing should leap down with it. When voicing a lead sheet, it is good to focus on voice leading when the melody doesn't move around too much. Don't worry when the melody leaps. Simply begin voice leading again when the melody returns to stepwise motion.

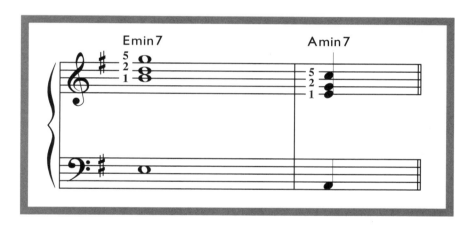

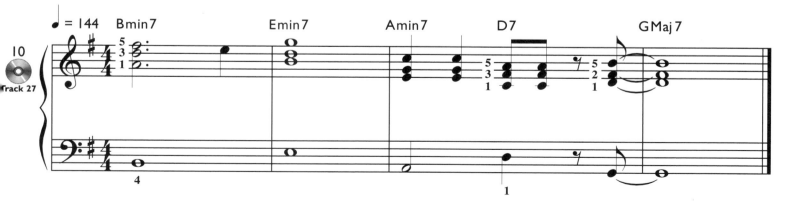

This is the lead sheet for *Bouncin' With Bill E.*, dedicated to the great Bill Evans. The changes are loosely based on the standard tune *I'll Remember April.* Learn it well because most of the remaining voicing lessons in this chapter will be based on this tune. Begin by voicing it

with roots in the left hand and 3rds, 5ths and 7ths (plus the melody note if it isn't already one of these) in the right hand. Check it against the written-out music on page 53. If you encounter a bar with rests instead of notes, simply voice the chord(s) however you see fit.

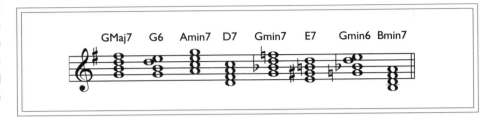

BOUNCIN' WITH BILL E. (LEAD SHEET)

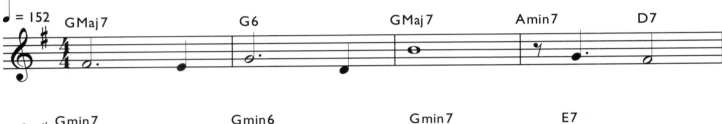

*Pianist **Bill Evans** was a master of harmony and improvisation. His work has been a source of inspiration to jazz musicians and fans since the 1950s.*

Here's a fully voiced version of *Bouncin' With Bill E.*. What you play from the lead sheet should be similar to this, but don't worry if there are voicings here and there that don't match exactly. You should be playing the correct notes in the chords, of course, but beyond that we can be somewhat flexible since there are many different ways to voice a chord.

BOUNCIN' WITH BILL E.

As the Declaration of Independence says, all people are created equal. The same can't be said for chord tones, however. Some are more important than others. Let's line up the three most common 7th chords (major, minor and dominant) from a root of D, and take a look:

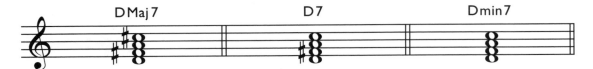

We know the root is important since that is what defines the chord. The 3rd and 7th are not the same from chord to chord so we need those to determine the chord quality. The 5th, however, is another story. The major, minor and dominant 7th chords all have perfect 5ths. That means we could leave the 5th out entirely and still know which of these three chords was being played.

To play *shell voicings*, we use the same concept we've been using but leave out the 5th of each chord; the roots go in the left hand and the right hand takes the 3rds and 7ths. If the melody note is the 3rd or 7th of a chord, we have three-note chords; if not, we add the melody note on top and have a four-note chord. Either way, this is a very sparse, compact way to voice chords without losing the character of the changes. Play this I-vi-ii-V-I in G Major.

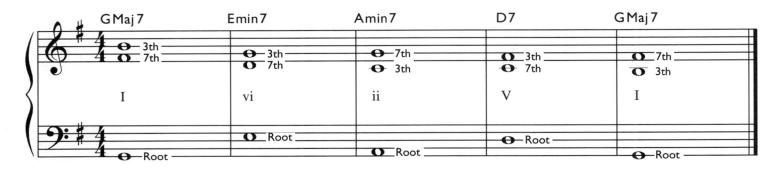

These voicings just get easier and easier on the hands, don't they? In the above example, the right hand barely has to move at all. This ease in voice leading is common with shell voicings whenever the roots are moving down in 5ths (or up in 4ths). In these cases, the most you'll have to move to get from the 7th of one chord to the 3rd of the next is a whole step, sometimes only a half step. To get from the 3rd of one chord to the 7th of the next, you often need only to repeat the same note!

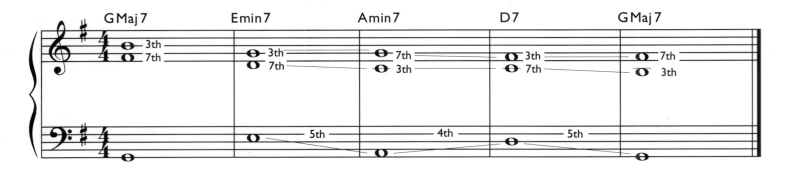

Here we have *Bouncin' With Bill E.* voiced with shells. Pay attention to the places where the 3rd or 7th is in the melody and only three notes are needed for the voicings. Since you won't have to move your hands much, use your extra energy to notice the smooth voice leading.

BOUNCIN' WITH BILL E. (SHELL VOICINGS)

BEBOP STYLE LEFT HAND VOICINGS

When we discussed soloing in Chapter 3, the examples divided the roles of the hands; the right hand soloed, the left hand played chords. This is a common division of labor in modern jazz keyboard. Earl "Fatha" Hines, Teddy Wilson and Nat "King" Cole were all pioneers in soloing with the right hand while allowing the left to fill in the harmony, and they usually did this with an ornate style of left hand voicing. In the *bebop* era (starting in the 1940s), horn players like trumpeter Dizzy Gillespie and saxophonist Charlie "Bird" Parker developed a new, exciting style of soloing. The solo lines in bebop tended to be so full of rhythmic and harmonic ideas that there was less need to fill in space with the left hand. Bebop pianists, led by Earl "Bud" Powell, began to use simple, skeletal voicings with their left hand, often with only two notes per chord.

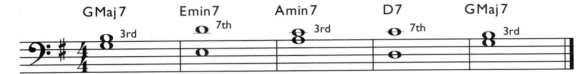

And we thought that shell voicings were sparse! Bebop style left hand voicings consist of either the root and 3rd or root and 7th of a chord. These voicings by themselves don't sound full enough to define the chords. Having just D and F♯ is not enough information to know that you have a D7 chord. However, when you combine these voicings in the left hand with melodies and solos in the right hand, the sound begins to fill out, and the left hand is better able to stay out of the right hand's way.

A great benefit of these voicings is improved voice leading. In Chapter 3, our left hands were jumping all over the place to get from one root position chord to the next but with triads we could get away with it. With 7th chords, that would be too clunky but the extra note gives us more voice leading options. To play bebop style voicings, think of "voicings on the half shell": shell voicings with one of the two non-root tones taken away. So if you play root-7th on one chord (and the root is going down a 5th), you'll play root-3rd on the next and vice-versa.

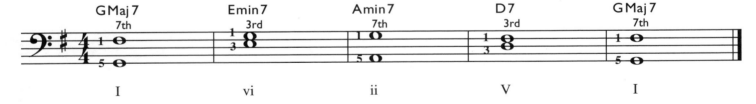

None of the notes in the above voicings go above the G below middle C which leaves the right hand plenty of room to solo without any overlapping of the hands. As long as you keep the non-root tones above the D below middle C, it shouldn't sound muddy.

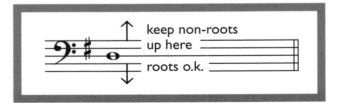

If you have big hands, one way to enrich the sound of bebop style voicings is by playing the root-3rd voicings with the root an octave lower. This gives you the interval of a 10th (an octave plus a 3rd), a fuller sound than the 3rd. If you feel an uncomfortable stretch when you reach a 10th, don't do it. It is not worth getting tendonitis to liven up your voicings.

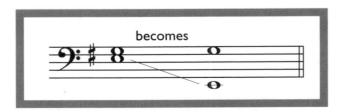

Bouncin' With Bill E. is found here with bebop style voicings in the left hand. To make things a little more interesting, the melody in the right hand is embellished a bit. Practice one hand at a time if you find it helpful. If your left hand can handle it, try stretching the 3rds into 10ths. Pay attention, as always, to the voice leading in the left hand.

BOUNCIN' WITH BILL E. *(BEBOP STYLE LEFT-HAND VOICINGS)*

Many inventions through time have given musicians the freedom to better express themselves. The invention of the phonograph allowed musicians to be recorded so that a piece could be listened to over and over. The invention of radio allowed musicians to be heard in places where they could never actually travel. And we jazz keyboardists should give a hearty pat on the back to whoever invented bass players!

With all the voicing types we've discussed so far, we've had to play the root in the left hand. Without the root down below, a chord usually sounds vague. But nobody said that we had to always be the ones playing the roots. Most jazz groups include a bassist (either bass guitar or acoustic "upright" bass), and usually the bassist's job is to keep a solid pulse and lay down the roots of the chords. We can leave the roots to the bassist and worry only about the rest of the notes.

Let's take the same I-vi-ii-V-I in G Major that we've used for the last couple of examples and look at it voiced with *rootless voicings* in the left hand.

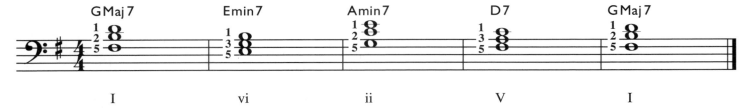

Here we begin with the same voicing concept that we introduced on pages 48 and 49, where we put the root on the bottom (with the left hand) and added the 3rd, 5th and 7th on top (with the right hand). Instead, though, we let the bass player take over the duties of the left hand and let the left hand play what the right hand would be playing. This leaves the right hand free to solo (or grab a sandwich, if so inclined).

The sound and feel of rootless voicings may take some getting used to, especially if you don't have the opportunity to play with a bassist. Have no fear, though. It will be very helpful to be comfortable with rootless voicings, and in time you will get used to the sound and hear the harmonic movement even if the roots aren't being played by anybody. For now, if you don't feel grounded as you play rootless voicings, slow down, hit the sustain pedal, and reach over with your right hand to play the roots underneath. Here are the changes for the first five bars of *Well, How About Bridgeport?* (page 50) voiced with left hand rootless voicings.

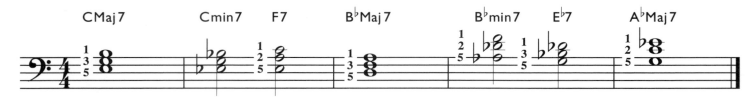

At the change from B♭Maj7 to B♭min7, the voicing leaps up rather than continuing the voice leading. This makes sense here since going below that D with anything but the root will muddy the sound, as we saw with bebop style voicings.

It is still possible to play root position chords with a bass player present, but the common technique in contemporary jazz is to let the bassist have the roots and stay out of his way. Rootless voicings can be a nice change of pace even in solo playing, and when you find yourself in an ensemble situation, you'll be very glad to know them.

Yet again, *Bouncin' With Bill E.*, this time with the right hand taking the melody and the left hand playing three note (3rd, 5th and 7th) rootless voicings underneath.

BOUNCIN' WITH BILL E. (ROOTLESS LEFT HAND VOICINGS)

Track 31

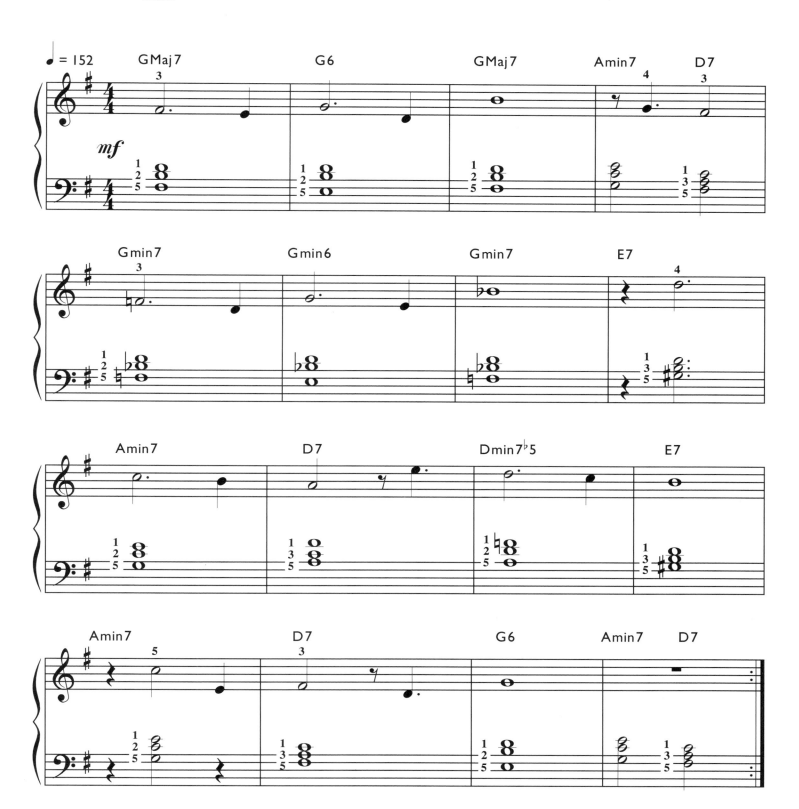

Rootless shell voicings are simply a combination of the concepts of rootless voicings and shell voicings. The left hand plays the 3rd and 7th of each chord, allowing the bassist to play the roots and giving the right hand freedom to do its thing.

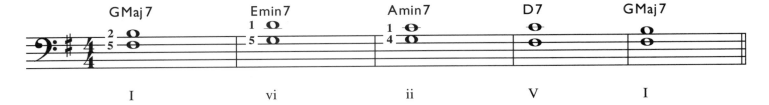

When we voiced these changes with shells on page 54, we used a different voicing for the Emin7. This version has the 7th on top in the Emin7 chord, whereas the one on page 54 had the 3rd on top. Either way is valid. Your goal is to voice the chord so that it is not too far below middle C, which would produce a muddy sound.

(muddy)

By looking ahead to the length of a progression and how much downward motion in 5ths you'll have, you can judge the range in which you should begin voicing to avoid the muddy notes and awkward leaps.

The one and only **Thelonious Monk,** *who thrived on sparse voicings like these, was often misunderstood and little known during his lifetime (1917-1982).*

Now that you can play the melody to *Bouncin' With Bill E.* in your sleep, we're going to make things more interesting in the left hand. The rendition below has the left hand playing rootless shell voicings. Rather than using half and whole notes, the rhythms are varied to closer resemble a typical left hand accompaniment. Work on the left hand separately if you need to, working out the syncopated rhythms precisely and with a good swing feel.

BOUNCIN' WITH BILL E. (*ROOTLESS SHELL VOICINGS*)

Track 32

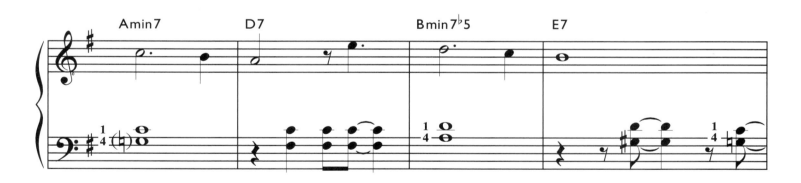

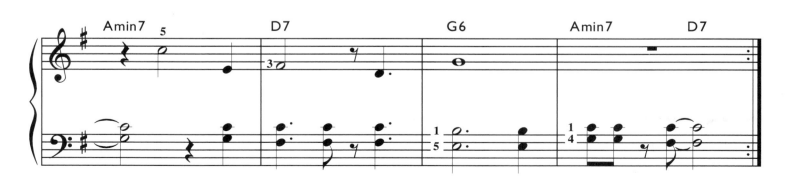

Comping is jazz lingo for the chordal accompaniment a pianist or guitarist provides during a melody or solo. Some say it is short for "accompanying" and some say it is short for "complementing." In fact, comping is both of those things. You can comp behind another player or you can use your left hand to comp for your right hand while you solo or play a melody.

The next time you listen to a jazz group, be aware of the comping. Some compers, like Horace Silver, take control of the music with their aggressive comping. Others, like Wynton Kelly, let the soloists take control, choosing instead to punctuate the soloists' statements. There are no hard and fast rules about what approach to take except one: listen! Your ears and sensitivity will be the keys to successful comping. If a soloist is playing softly and you're banging, something's wrong. Likewise, if the soloist is building a solo's energy level higher and higher and you're playing the same stuff you were two minutes ago, you're probably not listening. Great compers like Wynton Kelly, Red Garland, Cedar Walton and Kenny Barron often sound like mind readers. They listen to the soloist so well that they're always playing the right thing, and they can even predict where the soloist is going and comp accordingly.

Among the elements of good comping, good rhythm is about on a par with listening. The jazz *rhythm section* usually consists of bass, drums and keyboard (most often piano, sometimes organ, occasionally electric piano or synthesizer). Other possible rhythm section instruments include percussion, guitar and vibraphone. The rhythm section listens to and responds to the soloist, but first and foremost their job is to set a groove that feels great (refer to the explanation of swing feel on page 31). Compare the two examples below.

The first example is fine, especially in a laid back, reserved setting (for example, the saxophone solo has just begun softly and sparsely). The second example (with the same voicings but different rhythms) is much more propulsive and exciting, appropriate for a high energy situation. Syncopation (note especially how the Emin7 and D7 are anticipated by half a beat) adds a lot of drive to your comping. Listen attentively to the way the great compers do it and you'll get the sound in your head.

One more time! Here we have a sample solo over the changes to *Bouncin' With Bill E.* with the left hand comping underneath using the three types of left hand voicings we've studied. Learn each hand separately if you need to and pay close attention to the rhythms between the two hands. Sometimes the left hand emphasizes the rhythms that the right hand plays; other times the left hand punctuates where the right hand is less rhythmically active. Remember to swing!

BOUNCIN' WITH BILL E. *(SAMPLE SOLO WITH COMPING)*

Track 34

All Hail the King, dedicated to the great pianist Nat "King" Cole, is in the style of the changes to Kurt Weill's *Mack the Knife*. Louis Armstrong, Dick Hyman and Sonny Rollins are among those who have recorded great jazz versions of that tune. Here, we're in the key of A Major, and in sixteen bars we'll go through all the voicing types discussed in this chapter.

ALL HAIL THE KING

Track 35

Tommy's Touch, a tribute to pianist Tommy Flanagan, is presented here in lead sheet form. The tune uses harmony from the keys of B♭ Major and its relative, G Minor, which share the same key signature of two flats. Familiarize yourself with the melody and the changes. Then go through each voicing method discussed in this chapter and work out the tune with each method. This tune is in the style of the changes to the standard *Autumn Leaves*, which has been recorded successfully by the likes of Bill Evans, Erroll Garner and Julian "Cannonball" Adderley.

TOMMY'S TOUCH

CHAPTER 6

Scales and Soloing, Part Two

Now that we're using 7th chords, our sound is getting more colorful. Naturally we want our soloing to move forward as well. In this chapter we're not going to look at any scales we haven't already learned. Instead we're going to take the scales we already know and learn how to apply them in some new ways.

To prepare to dig into soloing, review all the scales we've looked at so far:

Major

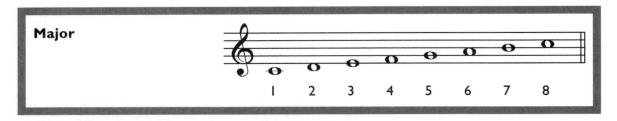

Major Pentatonic

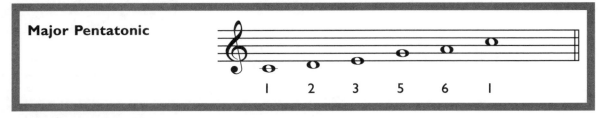

Natural Minor

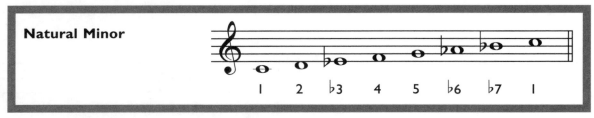

Harmonic Minor

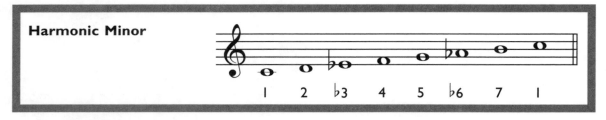

Minor Pentatonic

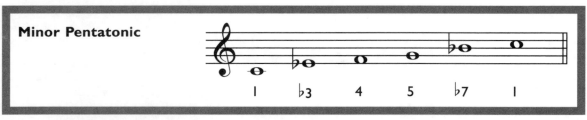

Blues

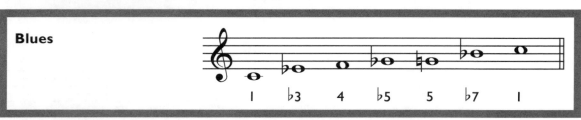

HARMONIC ANALYSIS

Harmonic analysis is taking a set of changes and figuring out what they mean. Let's say you open up a chart and see the following progression:

| Amin7 | Dmin7 | Gmin7 | C7 | FMaj7 | FMaj7 |

It is time for you to solo and you're trying to make heads or tails of the changes. Luckily, you have the chord chart from page 44 (perhaps by now you've tatooed it onto your arm) and scanning it, you realize that all these chords fit into the key of F Major. So, you take a pencil and jot down the key and the Roman numerals associated with each chord.

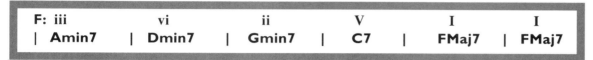

F: iii	vi	ii	V	I	I
Amin7	Dmin7	Gmin7	C7	FMaj7	FMaj7

Now you can go your merry way, soloing in F Major (using the F Major scale or the F Major Pentatonic scale) and keeping track of how the harmonic drama unfolds as the vi leads to ii which leads to V, and so on. Look for clues in the changes.

If you see a min7 moving to a 7 down a 5th, then you've got a ii-V, and that tells you (at least for the moment) what key you're in.

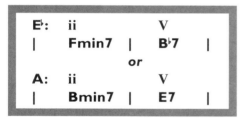

E♭:	ii	V
	Fmin7	B♭7

or

A:	ii	V
	Bmin7	E7

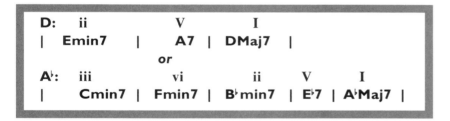

D:	ii	V	I
	Emin7	A7	DMaj7

or

A♭:	iii	vi	ii	V	I
	Cmin7	Fmin7	B♭min7	E♭7	A♭Maj7

If those same changes then go to a Maj7 chord down a 5th, that's a dead giveaway. The iii-vi-ii-V-I is another common pattern that makes it clear what key you're in.

The tunes in this chapter are examples of what you can do when you're in control of the changes and know where they come from. The left hand is given voicings and rhythms for comping but you're encouraged to play around with them, trying different voicings and rhythms for more personalized comping. Most importantly, have fun noodling around with the scales and chords. Improvising is loads of fun, and you should enjoy the opportunity to play your own melodies as they come into your head.

The melody and changes to *Pebble Hill* are based on the A Major scale. Learn the melody and use the A Major scale to solo. You can use the written comping pattern or use your own. Keep swinging the eighth notes but since the tune is in $\frac{3}{4}$ time, there is a slight difference to the rhythmic feel (you can't emphasize the two and four if there is no four!). The written left hand part shows examples of typical $\frac{3}{4}$ rhythms. The parentheses around the final E7 imply that you should use that change on a turnaround to bring you back to the top of the tune, but when you end the tune leave it out and end on the AMaj7.

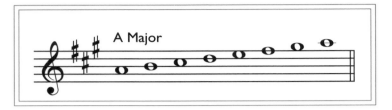

PEBBLE HILL

Track 37

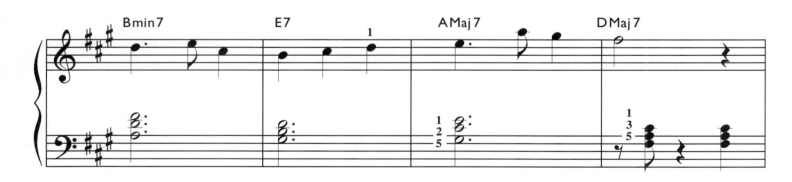

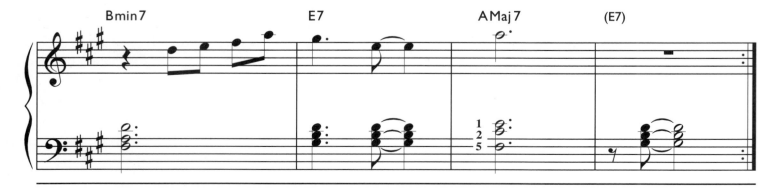

Brother Jack is dedicated to the intensely swingin' organists Jack McDuff and Shirley Scott. It's in the key of E♭ Major, and the melody is derived entirely from the E♭ Major Pentatonic scale, so you can try soloing just from that scale. The song is in AABA form.

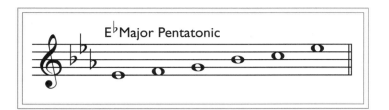

BROTHER JACK AND SISTER SHIRLEY

Fine

D.C. al Fine
(no repeat)

Just as there are ways to tell what major key you're in, the same opportunity exists for minor keys. Let's start by looking at this progression:

| | B♭Maj7 | | FMaj7 | | Emin7♭5 | | A7 | | Dmin7 | ‖

Because the first chord is B♭Maj7, we might instinctively assume that we're in the key of B♭ major. But in jazz harmony, where you start is less important that where you're going. As the progression moves further along we see it moving us to Dmin7 and realize that all the chords relate to the key of D Minor.

Dmin: VI   **III**   **ii**   **V**   **i**
| **B♭Maj7** | **FMaj7** | **Emin7♭5** | **A7** | **Dmin7** ‖

As with major keys, there are certain chord patterns in minor keys that clearly point you towards recognizing the key.

If you see a min7♭5 chord moving down a 5th to a 7th chord, that is a sign you're in a minor key.

Emin: ii   V
| F♯min7♭5 | B7 |

If you have the same progression and the 7 chord goes down a 5th to a min7 or min6 chord, then it is even more clear that you're in a minor key.

B♭min: ii   V   I
| Cmin7♭5 | F7 | B♭min6 |

If you see a Maj7 chord move down a half step to a dominant chord, that is another good sign that a 5th below the 7th chord lies the i chord in the present minor key.

Fmin: VI   V   (i)
| D♭Maj7 | C7 | (Fmin7) |

Sometimes a tune passes freely between relative major and minor keys, like *Tommy's Touch* on page 65, which goes back and forth between B♭ Major and its relative minor, G Minor. This makes which key we're in a bit more ambiguous. Not to worry, though, you can change your thinking whenever the changes hint more at one than the other. This will be addressed further on page 74 when we discuss modulations and pivot chords.

Tommy's Touch
E♭:   ii   V   I   IV   Cmin: ii   V   i
| Fmin7 | B♭7 | E♭Maj7 | A♭Maj7 | Dmin7♭5 | G7 | Cmin7 ‖

Blue Drew is in the key of B Minor and the melody uses the B Minor Pentatonic scale and the B Blues scale. The only difference is the F natural in the B Blues scale. These scales give us a funky, blues-based sound. Use each of these scales when you solo. Then begin to mix them up, adding the ♭5 from the blues scale when the mood strikes. This tune is dedicated to Kenny Drew who was one of the great pianists of modern jazz and an expert at this type of funky playing.

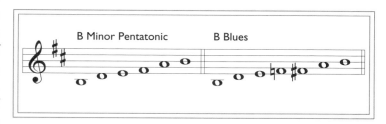

BLUE DREW

Track 39

We know by now that the harmony in a minor key is derived from the harmonic minor scale, but with some significant borrowing from the natural minor for certain chords. When it comes time to solo over a minor progression, the issue of which scale to use arises. Let's compare the two, using the first chord progression from page 70, voiced in the left hand with three-note rootless voicings. If we run the D Natural Minor scale over these changes, it sounds like this:

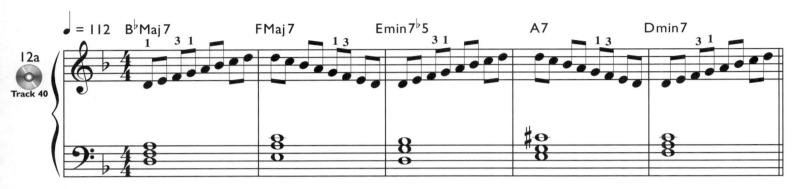

Not bad, but when we get to the ii-V, there is a little problem. The C# in the A7 chord, a crucial part of the progression, clashes with the C natural in the D Natural Minor scale. So now let's try the D Harmonic Minor scale, which has the missing C# we seek.

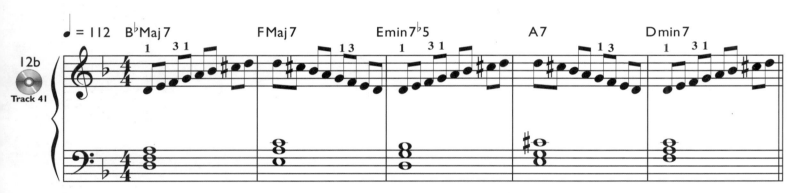

With this scale we solve one problem but add two more. The C# that we needed for the A7 clashes with the C naturals in the FMaj7 and Dmin7 chords.

The solution is to be flexible. If you want to use these scales, use the harmonic minor whenever you encounter a V or ii-V, and use the natural minor the rest of the time. This way you can "make the changes" (play melodies that match up with the chords going by).

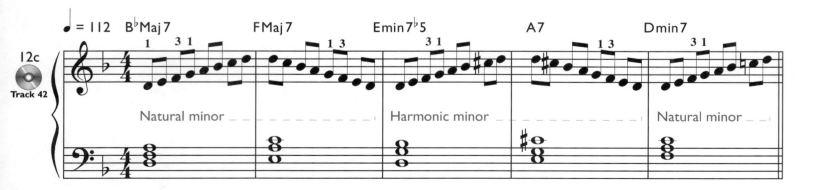

Mingus Reincarnated, a tribute to the great bassist/composer/bandleader Charles Mingus, is in the key of G Minor. The natural and harmonic minor are both used, changing wherever it is appropriate. When you solo, use the same scales as in the melody.

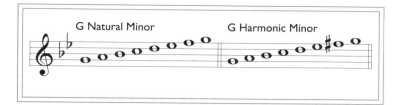

MINGUS REINCARNATED

Track 43

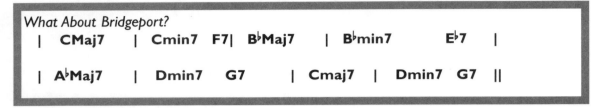

PROGRESSIONS WITH MODULATIONS

So you've decided to go back and try soloing on some of the tunes that came earlier in this book. Go back to page 50 and try to solo on the changes to *Well, How About Bridgeport?*

What About Bridgeport?

| CMaj7 | Cmin7 F7| B♭Maj7 | B♭min7 E♭7 |

| A♭Maj7 | Dmin7 G7 | Cmaj7 | Dmin7 G7 ||

The key signature has no sharps or flats and the first chord is CMaj7, so it seems like it is in C Major. But starting on the second measure, many of the chords don't fit with C Major. What you're encountering is *modulation*, the changing of keys. *Well, How About Bridgeport?* begins in C Major but it doesn't stay there. Look at the harmonic analysis for these changes:

What About Bridgeport?

C: I   B♭: ii   V   I   A♭: ii   V

| CMaj7 | Cmin7   F7 | B♭Maj7 | B♭min7   E♭7 |

    I   C: ii   V   I   ii   V

| A♭Maj7 | Dmin7   G7 | CMaj7 | Dmin7   G7 ||

So actually the tune passes through the keys of C Major, B♭ Major and A♭ Major. No one scale is going to work soloing over the whole tune. You can use the major (or major pentatonic) scale that corresponds with each key while you're there, and then move on to the next when it's time.

Sometimes, as in *Tommy's Touch*, there is an overlap of chords as the modulation occurs.

Tommy's Touch

E♭:   ii   V   I   IV   vii   Cmin: V   i
or
Cmin: iv   VII   III   VI   ii   V   i

| Fmin7 | B♭7 | E♭Maj7 | A♭Maj7 | Dmin7♭5 | G7 | Cmin7 ||

The first five chords in this progression could be analyzed as relating to either of the two keys, E♭ Major and C Minor. These chords are examples of *pivot chords*. A pivot chord is a chord that functions in two keys and helps provide a smooth transition in the modulation from one key to the next. When pivot chords arise, you have a choice whether to think in the key you're coming from or the one you're going to. Either is fine, as long as you're prepared for the modulation.

The key to modulation is awareness. Stay on your toes as a tune goes along and keep looking out for cues that will help you determine what key you're in at that moment. Once you've determined that you're temporarily in a certain key, you can do the same things to solo that you would do if you were in that key for a whole tune.

Bright Red was composed in memory of pianist Red Garland. This tune modulates repeatedly. The melody is derived from the major scale of whichever key the tune is in at a given moment. Use this tune to practice your ability to quickly shift gears as your solo accounts for each modulation by changing the scale you use.

BRIGHT RED

You Neeque uses in the syle of the standard tunes *There Will Never Be Another You* and *You're a Weaver of Dreams*. These changes modulate repeatedly, usually using pivot chords for smooth transitions. Learn the tune, familiarizing yourself with the changes and the keys the tune passes through. Whenever pivot chords come up, the primary chord symbol is from the key the chord is leading to. The chord symbols in parentheses indicate the functions of the chords if you relate them to the key you're leaving (the key you were just in).

YOU NEEQUE

Track 45

Here's a sample chorus-long solo over the changes to *You Neeque* using scales appropriate to the keys through which the tune passes.

YOU NEEQUE (SAMPLE SOLO)

Track 46

MEMORIZING CHANGES

In addition to guiding your scale choices for a solo, harmonic analysis is an indispensable tool in helping you memorize changes. Imagine if you had to memorize directions to a place one word at a time: "Go . . . down . . . the . . . block . . . and . . . ." Similarly, if we had to memorize the changes to the A-section of *Well, How About Bridgeport* by thinking "C Major 7 to C Minor 7 to F7 . . ." our brains would run out of space long before we got to the end of the tune. By using Roman numerals, we can condense changes into bigger chunks of information. Instead of thinking of each chord one at a time, we can think:

"I in C to ii-V-I in B♭ to ii-V-I in A♭ to ii-V-I in C . . ."

Here we just took ten chords and condensed them into four pieces of information to remember. As we get used to common chord progressions, it will be easier to condense the information in the same way that we think of "Take a left at the stop sign" as one piece of information and not seven.

Oscar Peterson,
often compared with Art Tatum,
was born in Montreal in 1925.
His most popular trio included .
Herb Ellis (guitar) and Ray
Brown (double bass).

TRANSPOSING CHANGES

Another way in which Roman numerals help is with transposition, playing something in another key. Unless you plan to always keep one hand on the "pitch modulation" button of your synthesizer, this is a skill worth developing. Sometimes a singer's voice range doesn't fit the key you're used to using; sometimes somebody will just want to play something in a different key. Let's say somebody wants to play *Well, How About Bridgeport* in F Major. Instead of trying to of bring every chord up a 4th, think of the Roman numerals. We know we have I in the home key, followed by ii-V-I down a whole step, ii-V-I down another whole step and then ii-V-I back in the home key. In F, that would be:

F: I	E♭: ii	V	I	D♭: ii	V	I	F: ii	V	I
| FMaj7	| Fmin7	B♭7	| E♭Maj7	| E♭min7	A♭7	| D♭maj7	| Gmin7	C7	| FMaj7 ||

Señor Ruiz, dedicated to pianist Hilton Ruiz, is a tune with a Latin feel, so play the eighth notes straight (don't swing them). The changes are in the style of the harmony from the modern jazz classic *Blue Bossa* by trumpeter Kenny Dorham. On this tune, learn (and try to memorize) the changes based on the Roman numerals. Notice that it modulates from C Minor up a half step to D♭ Major. Once you have it down, slowly work on transposing it into the other eleven keys. You can choose the keys by going up or down in half steps or by going around the circle of 5ths (see page 11 if you need help remembering the circle).

SEÑOR RUIZ

Track 47

CHAPTER 7

More Soloing

MELODIC SCALE PATTERNS

If someone says "don't forget that this weekend is Groundhog Day," you may or may not remember. If a little while later, they say "remember this weekend," you'll be more likely to remember. *Repetition* is a great tool in jazz improvisation as well, allowing you to make the most out of every musical idea and giving listeners something to latch onto so that they'll remember your musical statements.

Melodic scale patterns are a good source of musical repetition. Most musicians practice patterns like these as technical exercises.

The *Virtuoso Pianist* by Hanon (Alfred #616), used by many keyboard students, is a book of technical exercises based on these sorts of patterns. There are many other books like it. If you played the above examples verbatim over a tune in C Major, it would sound . . . well, boring. Kind of like hearing "Don't forget Groundhog Day" every minute for an hour, which would probably make you less interested in groundhogs after a while. Therefore, we have to be a bit creative about how we dress up the patterns to keep them interesting (see the exercise on the next page). Still, practicing straight patterns can be a technical and musical boost, even if you're not going to play them verbatim in a solo. You're encouraged to check out Hanon or another pattern book and use it to build your chops and give you some ideas for patterns to play.

Here we use the pattern from the previous page, example ①, with the C Major scale. The pattern is kept intact but the rhythm in which it is played is varied throughout, and it is used over repeated ii-V-I's in C. This serves as an introduction to using patterns creatively in a jazz context. Voice the changes in the left hand in whatever style you like.

*Born in 1928, **Horace Silver** is a prolific composer. His use of blues and gospel devices in jazz has made him one of our most influential players.*

ARPEGGIOS

An *arpeggio* is a "broken chord." We've been playing all the notes in our chords simultaneously (*block chords*) but we can also *arpeggiate* the chords and play one note at a time.

Arpeggios give us yet another melodic possibility when we solo. They are particularly useful in "making the changes." Playing scales over a progression addresses the key of the changes but not necessarily the individual chord. Arpeggios, on the other hand, lay out the sound of each and every chord that is arpeggiated.

The principles of voice leading are still very important when playing arpeggios in a jazz solo. Compare these two arpeggiations of a iii-vi-ii-V-I in E♭ Major.

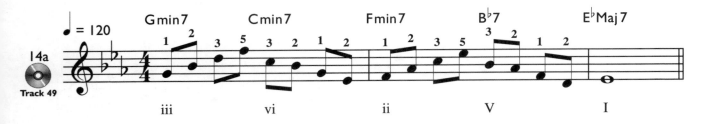

In example 14a, each arpeggio begins with the root, but there are awkward leaps from the Gmin7 to the Cmin7 and from the Fmin7 to the B♭7. In example 14b, a nearby chord tone is played at every chord change, resulting in a smoother sound. Practice the smooth linking of arpeggios over whatever changes you're trying to solo on.

As with patterns, smooth can be dull after a certain point. Once you're able to smoothly link arpeggios, you can throw in some leaps to mix things up.

The three exercises that follow all use the same changes, ii-V-I's going counterclockwise around the circle of 5ths (therefore making it a circle of 4ths) through all twelve major keys. Practice the right hand alone at first so you can get used to hearing the sound of the changes from the arpeggios themselves. Once you're comfortable with the right hand, you can choose your own left hand voicings to play underneath.

This exercise deals with the smooth linking of arpeggios. Remember to swing those eighth notes; just because it is an exercise doesn't mean it shouldn't swing.

This exercise keeps the same constant eighth-note rhythm and the same goal of smoothly linking the arpeggios. Although the arpeggios lead smoothly into one another and only chord tones are played, there is more freedom to the melodic contour, compared to the "straight up and down" nature of the last exercise.

This exercise is freer still, allowing for rhythmic variety as well as variety in melodic contour. The sound gets more and more musical and we're still only using chord tones.

It is very difficult to play an engaging solo using just one technique. Scales, chords, arpeggios and melodic patterns can all be interesting and musical, but after a couple choruses of any one of them, boredom is likely to set in. Using all of these elements in a single solo makes it much easier to keep things interesting. Let's look at a I-vi-ii-V-I in G Major using several different elements.

The G Major scale

All of these sound fine, but let's extend the progression (by repeating it once) and try using all of these elements.

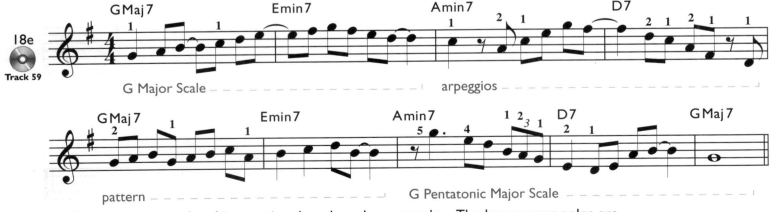

This is more varied and interesting than the other examples. The longer your solos are, the more important it is to have this kind of variety to maintain interest.

We're going to take a more in-depth look at how to combine the elements we've studied in this book, using the tune *Wonder-ful* as the basis. *Wonder-ful* is in the style of the progression in Stevie Wonder's *You Are the Sunshine Of My Life*, which has been recorded in a jazz style by the likes of Mal Waldron, Phineas Newborn, Jr. and Ella Fitzgerald. Learn the tune well, especially the changes, before moving on to the next few pages. In pencil, write out a harmonic analysis over the chords in this lead sheet.

WONDER-FUL
Track 60

Here is a sample solo over a chorus of *Wonder-ful* using a variety of elements. Once you've learned this solo, try taking your own solo using the same elements. Try choosing for yourself which elements you're going to use where. There are no wrong choices, so explore!

(SAMPLE SOLO #1 ON) WONDER-FUL
Track 61

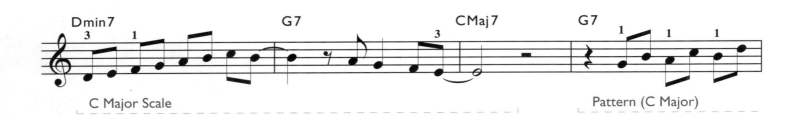

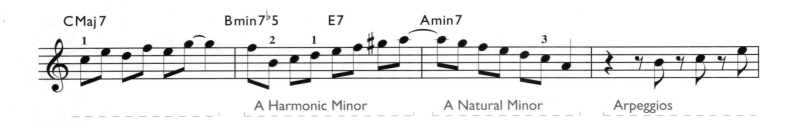

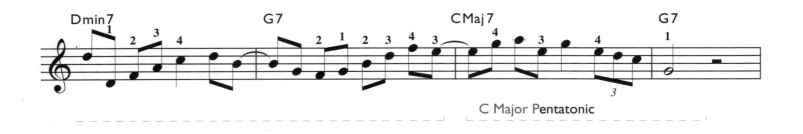

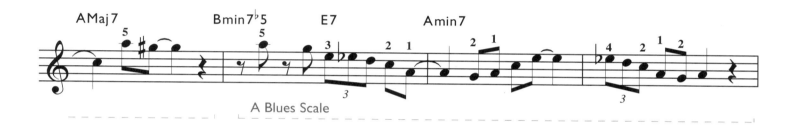

* The C# in the seventh measure of the second page of this tune is in the B Minor scale, but is not a member of the Bmin7 chord being arpeggiated at the moment. This kind of mixture of scale and arpeggio is common in jazz.

Here is another solo chorus on *Wonder-ful*, still using a variety of elements. This time the focus is on the left hand. Dig into the left hand here, noticing the types of voicings used, the rhythms and the way the comping interacts with the solo.

(SAMPLE SOLO #2 ON) *WONDER-FUL* (WITH COMPING)

CHAPTER 8

Afterword

EAR TRAINING

You may have thought that the fingers were the most important part of a jazz keyboardist's anatomy. Fingers are near the top of the list, definitely, but the ears win out. The tradition of jazz is an aural tradition and even if we use written music, we are always depending on our ears. *Ear training* is the practice of learning to hear things. A seasoned jazz musician can hear just about anything whether at the keyboard or away from it. Here are some ways to practice your ear training.

1) **Practice identifying sounds.** If you hear the interval of a minor 2nd, do you recognize it? How about a min7♭5 chord? If the answer is no, not really or sometimes, this would be useful to practice. Focus on one thing at a time — intervals, triads, 7th chords, chord progressions, etc. Have a friend play different intervals (or whatever you're focusing on) and try to identify them. If you don't have anyone else around, record examples on a tape recorder or sequencer and wait a few days until you've forgotten what you played. Or simply pop in a CD or turn on the radio and try to figure out what is going on by ear. Strive for a level where it is second nature to be able to hear and identify anything.

2) **Play along.** Put on an album you like and play along with it. Don't worry about getting every note or even most of them. Just practice hearing things and trying to play them back instantly. After a while your ability to recreate what you hear will improve. Anything you want to play along with is fine, as long as it is not so fast and complex that you can't keep up. Particularly useful is playing along with improvisations on tunes you already know.

3) **Transcribe.** Take a recording of a solo or some chord voicings that you particularly like. Begin by listening several times so that the sound is firmly in your head and all you need to do is figure out what the notes are. Then sit down at the keyboard with the recording and figure out exactly what they're doing. You can write it down or try to memorize it right from the record. You will gain some insight into that player's style, and instead of blowing fifteen bucks on a transcription, you'll have the satisfaction of knowing you did it yourself and improved your ears in the process.

4) **Sight sing.** Take a lead sheet to a tune you don't know. Give yourself the starting pitch at the keyboard and see if you can sing the rest. When your ears are well developed, this will be perfectly natural.

> **Note:**
>
> In many music magazines there are advertisements for methods of attaining *perfect pitch*. Perfect pitch is the ability to identify any note out of thin air. *Relative pitch,* on the other hand, is the ability to hear the relationships between notes. With relative pitch, you may not immediately know what the first note of a melody is, but if someone tells you, you can figure out the rest of the notes by how they sound in relation to the first one and to each other. Perfect pitch can certainly help but relative pitch is much more useful to a jazz musician.

TYPES OF KEYBOARDS

"Keyboard" can have many different meanings. Traditionally, the acoustic piano is by far the most common jazz keyboard instrument. Coming in second is the organ — in the 1950s, Jimmy Smith and others legitimized the Hammond B-3 as a modern jazz instrument. In the '60s and '70s, people began to experiment with electric pianos like the Wurlitzer and the Fender Rhodes. Then, beginning in the '70s, more jazz musicians began to use synthesizers. Affordable synthesizers were eventually built that tried to simulate the sounds and effects of the more traditional instruments. These are still popular.

Nowadays, we have several options for keyboards to play and/or purchase.

1) **Acoustic piano.** After all these years, the piano is still the King of Keyboards in straight-ahead jazz. The tone, touch and responsiveness of a good piano are unmatched. On the downside, a good piano is neither cheap nor portable. Therefore, many contemporary keyboardists find themselves looking at other options in addition to or instead of pianos.

2) **Organ.** A Hammond B-3 is cheaper and more portable than a piano, but not by much. Also, since the sound of the organ is less common than that of the piano, investing in an organ means committing to that sound.

3) **Electric piano.** You or someone you know may own an old Fender Rhodes and you can probably find one in the want ads pretty cheap. They are heavy but portable enough to take to a gig and the touch and responsiveness are often great. The sound of the Rhodes and other electric (not electronic) pianos, however, seems to scream "70s!" If you and the people you're playing with don't have a problem with this, then it might not be a bad choice. Another thing to keep in mind is that most electric pianos are no longer manufactured so getting them repaired can be difficult.

4) **Digital piano.** Many companies now manufacture digital pianos. The sounds are similar to piano sounds, the feel (with weighted "piano-like" keys) is similar to a piano and it is cheaper and more portable than a piano. These instruments aren't quite the "real thing," but all things considered, they're often worthy substitutes.

5) **Synthesizer.** There is a broad range of synthesizers out there with a range of prices and capabilities. For the sake of playing jazz, the most important feature is touch sensitivity (having the dynamic level of a note change depending on how hard you hit the key). Without that, it is hard to play jazz expressively. If you can get weighted or semi-weighted keys, that is helpful, too. Another important feature is having enough polyphony (notes you can play at once) to not run out of notes when you play big chords or use the sustain pedal. It is hard to get by with less than sixteen note polyphony. Finally, sounds are important but so many affordable MIDI (Musical Instrument Digital Interface) modules are available with good sounds that you can always upgrade your sounds later on, as long as your synth is MIDI compatible.

TUNES

If you are comfortable with most of the concepts in this book, you are ready to learn some tunes.

You should save a few dollars and buy yourself a *fake book*. A fake book (sometimes called a "real book") is a book of lead sheets to commonly played tunes.

Fake books can be found at virtually any music store. Sometimes the tunes are typeset and easy to read, other times they are handwritten. The charts vary from painstakingly accurate to thumbnail sketches. No book of this type tries to put all the tunes you will ever need into one book, emphasizing quality over quantity.

Build a library of tune sources. This way you can cross-reference between books to figure out the "correct" way to play a tune. If you can only get one fake book, the choice depends on your needs.

Once you have some tunes, PLAY THEM. Go to some jazz gigs and jam sessions and see what tunes people are playing. If you hear a particular tune often, learn it. If there is a tune that keeps showing up on records you have, learn it. If you don't have a lead sheet, ask a musician who knows it to show it to you. Or, if your ears are up to the task, try taking the tune off a record. Begin by trying to hear the roots in the bass. Then, see if you can figure out the changes. Go back and figure out the melody.

Also, try sight-reading lead sheets out of fake books. See if you can quickly (if not necessarily perfectly) take a tune you don't already know and play the melody, the chords and a solo. This way you will be exposed to more tunes and you will get into the practice of sight reading tunes. When you play with other people, you are likely to play tunes you don't already know and it is very useful to be able to read them like this.

Make tunes a focal point of your jazz education. When you learn a new concept or technique, try applying it to a tune. Make it a goal to learn enough tunes so that you can go out and play with other people. Playing with other people is where you will get your most important training.

RECORDINGS

The following is a list of recordings that are well worth checking out. This is not a comprehensive list by any means. These albums are simply a good place to start listening to great jazz. These recordings will help reinforce the ideas from this book. Enjoy!

— Cannonball Adderley: *Somethin' Else* (with Hank Jones on piano)
— Louis Armstrong and Earl Hines: *Louis Armstrong and Earl Hines*
— Kenny Barron: *Wanton Spirit*
— Count Basie: *The Complete Count Basie on Decca*
— Count Basie: *The Atomic Basie*
— Art Blakey and the Jazz Messengers: *Three Blind Mice* (with Cedar Walton on piano)
— John Coltrane: *Blue Train* (with Kenny Drew on piano)
— Miles Davis: *Milestones* (with Red Garland on piano)
— Miles Davis: *In A Silent Way* (with Chick Corea, Herbie Hancock and Joe Zawinul on keyboards)
— Duke Ellington: *Piano Reflections*
— Duke Ellington: *Duke Ellington at Newport*
— Bill Evans: *Portrait in Jazz*
— Erroll Garner: *Concert By the Sea*
— Stan Getz: *Sweet Rain* (with Chick Corea on piano)
— Dexter Gordon: *A Swingin' Affair* (with Sonny Clark on piano)
— Herbie Hancock: *Takin' Off*
— Ahmad Jamal: *But Not For Me – Live at the Pershing*
— Jo Jones: *Jo Jones Trio* (with Ray Bryant on piano – also available as part of *The Essential Jo Jones*)
— Wynton Kelly Trio with Wes Montgomery: *Smokin' at the Half Note*
— Ramsey Lewis: *The In Crowd*
— Les McAnn and Eddie Harris: *Swiss Movement*
— Thelonious Monk: *Monk's Dream*
— Phineas Newborn, Jr.: *A World of Piano*
— Oscar Peterson Trio: *We Get Requests*
— Bud Powell: *The Genius of Bud Powell*
— Sonny Rollins: *Saxophone Colossus* (with Tommy Flanagan on piano)
— Horace Silver: *Finger Poppin'*
— Jimmy Smith: *Organ Grinder Swing*
— McCoy Tyner: *Inception*
— Art Tatum: *Piano Starts Here*
— Lester Young and Teddy Wilson: *Pres and Teddy*

Dig into any of these albums you can get your hands (and ears) on, and enjoy! We'll meet again in *Intermediate Jazz Keyboard*.